TWAYNE'S WORLD AUTHORS SERIES

A Survey of the World's Literature

Sylvia E. Bowman, Indiana University

GENERAL EDITOR

FRANCE

Maxwell A. Smith, Guerry Professor of French, Emeritus
The University of Chattanooga
Former Visiting Professor in Modern Languages
The Florida State University

EDITOR

Hippolyte Taine

(*TWAS 139*)

TWAYNE'S WORLD AUTHORS SERIES (TWAS)

The purpose of TWAS is to survey the major writers—novelists, dramatists, historians, poets, philosophers, and critics—of the nations of the world. Among the national literatures covered are those of Australia, Canada, China, Eastern Europe, France, Germany, Greece, India, Italy, Japan, Latin America, the Netherlands, New Zealand, Poland, Russia, Scandinavia, Spain, and the African nations, as well as Hebrew, Yiddish, and Latin Classical literatures. This survey is complemented by Twayne's United States Authors Series and English Authors Series.

The intent of each volume in these series is to present a critical-analytical study of the works of the writer; to include biographical and historical material that may be necessary for understanding, appreciation, and critical appraisal of the writer; and to present all material in clear, concise English—but not to vitiate the scholarly content of the work by doing so.

Hippolyte Taine

By LEO WEINSTEIN

Stanford University

Twayne Publishers, Inc. :: New York

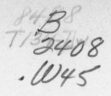

Preface

A new look at Taine has been necessary for a long time. How could so powerful and influential a thinker be neglected to the point of being dismissed with a shrug of the shoulder even by those who have never read a line by him? How could one of the most ambitious intellectual enterprises of the nineteenth century, the attempt to apply scientific methods to art, literature, psychology and history, be termed a failure without a thorough examination of its merits, shortcomings, and possible emendations? These puzzling questions are considered in the concluding chapter of this study.

In the thirty-five volumes or so that make up Hippolyte Taine's works and correspondence it would be easy to find any number of opposing views expressed during forty-five years of an intense intellectual life. Critics find him either highly inconsistent or else they insist on the unity of his ideas. The limits of this study make it impossible to point out all the complexities present in the living thought of a man who expresses himself in striking formulas, which are later completed by explanations and modifications, or who is occasionally so carried away by the impetus of an argument that he forgets what he has written previously.

The solution adopted here is to expose the persistent and recurring ideas and attitudes in Taine that withstood the vicissitudes of changing conditions or the moods of a moment. A typical example is the case of Racine, the great seventeenth-century French playwright. Taine criticized him severely in an early essay, but in a later work he raised him to the stature of the representative writer of a century the spirit of which he condemned elsewhere; then again he praised Racine in order to bury the English Restoration playwrights who imitated French Classical theater. Does this mean Taine had changed his mind since his first essay on Racine? Not at all. The answer becomes obvious once we realize the purpose Taine was pursuing in each particular case.

Since Taine hitched his star to science, the rank accorded to each of his amazingly varied fields of endeavor has been subject to the fluctuations in the prestige and progress of science itself.

Today his psychological treatise, a pioneer work at the time, happens to hold least importance; his voluminous historical study of modern France has been superseded by more recent works, although it still needs to be considered in any effort to interpret the French Revolution; his philosophical writings are both historically important and supply the basis for an understanding of his method. But the part of Taine's production that has best stood the test of time is his criticism of literature and art which combines a clearly exposed method, critical insights, and brilliance of style. To this, therefore the most space has been devoted. Questions of influence and highly technical matters have usually been assigned to footnotes.

Whenever possible I have attempted to deal with Taine on his own terms by first exposing the problems he had to solve, then explaining the method employed by him, next testing its validity, and finally examining in what manner and how faithfully he applied it to the particular subject under consideration. When his conclusions give rise to doubt, I have tried to determine what may have caused this problem by reviewing the process which led him to these conclusions.

Contrary to most critics in the past who claim that Taine was an excellent critic *in spite of* his method, my opinion is that he was not merely a first-rate critic but that his method, although it now needs additions and modifications, contributed greatly to his success. In fact, Taine is at his best when he sticks close to his method, as he did in his celebrated articles on Balzac and Stendhal.

For the past three years I have been living with Hippolyte Taine (to make up for this infidelity, the book is dedicated to my wife) and I can sincerely say that he has been splendid company. He states his method and his goal in a straightforward manner so that in case of disagreement one can say to him: "Let us check the facts, sir." He was one of the most cultured and civilized men of modern France and his manner of presenting his views always stimulates the mind, regardless of whether one agrees or not. I hope the reader will find him as challenging and rewarding as I have.

I wish to express my gratitude to Dr. James D. Ray for scientific advice, to Professor Philip Dawson of Stanford University for historical documentation; and to Father Jacques Pohier of Paris, France, and to Dr. Robert-Peter Aby of Berkeley, California, for generously placing at my disposal hard-to-find editions of Taine's works.

L.W.

Palo Alto, California

Contents

Preface

Chronology

1. The Man and His Times ..   15

2. Philosophy, Method and Psychology   28

3. The Literary Critic   51

4. Race, Milieu, Moment   80

5. The Art Critic   100

6. The Historian   122

7. Taine's Achievements and Influence   143

Notes and References   153

Selected Bibliography   169

Index   175

Chronology

1828   Hippolyte-Adolphe Taine is born in Vouziers (Ardennes), France, April 21.

1839   He is sent to Rethel (Ardennes) for private lessons with a priest.

1840   His father dies.

1841   Taine sent to Paris to study at a private school and at the Lycée Bourbon. He makes friends with Prévost-Paradol.

1848   He enters the Ecole Normale in Paris after having placed first in the entrance examinations.

1851   He is failed in the examination for the *agrégation*. He is appointed substitute philosophy teacher at the College of Nevers. Refuses to sign an oath of loyalty to Napoleon III.

1852   Taine is appointed substitute teacher of rhetoric at the College of Poitiers. Transferred to teach a lower class at Besançon, he asks for a leave and returns to Paris where he gives private lessons and attends courses at the Faculty of Medicine.

1853   Taine obtains his doctorate in letters. Publication: *Essay on La Fontaine's Fables*.

1855   *A Tour Through the Pyrenees* is published by Hachette. His *Essay on Livy* receives the prize of the French Academy. He begins to write articles of literary criticism for important magazines.

1857   *The Nineteenth Century French Philosophers* creates a sensation by attacking the reigning philosophers, especially Victor Cousin.

1858   *Critical and Historical Essays,* a collection of Taine's articles. Trip to Belgium, Holland, and Germany.

1860   First trip to England.

1861 *La Fontaine and His Fables,* a complete revision of his doctoral thesis. He begins a novel, *Etienne Mayran,* which will remain unfinished.

1862 Second trip to England.

1863 Taine is appointed admissions examiner at the Military Academy of Saint-Cyr.

1864 Trip to Italy. The first three volumes of his *History of English Literature* are presented to the French Academy, but no prize is awarded. He begins his courses as professor of esthetics and art history at the Ecole des Beaux-Arts in Paris.

1865 *New Critical and Historical Essays,* a collection of articles including his important essays on Racine, Balzac, and Stendhal.

1866 *Trip to Italy* is published.

1867 *Notes on Paris,* witty and biting comments on social life in Paris.

1868 Taine marries Mlle. Denuelle.

1869 Trip to Germany, Switzerland, and Italy.

1870 *On Intelligence,* Taine's treatise on psychology. Trip to Germany. Recalled to France by death in family. When war with Prussia breaks out, he offers his services but is rejected because of poor health.

1871 Taine lectures on Corneille and Racine at Oxford University, England, where he receives an honorary doctorate.

1872 *Notes on England* is published. Buys country home at Menthon-Saint-Bernard (Savoie), near the Lake of Annecy. He unsuccessfully presents his candidacy to the French Academy. He begins work on *The Origins of Contemporary France,* which will occupy him until his death.

1875 *The Ancien Régime* is published. The volumes of *The French Revolution* will appear in 1878, 1881, and 1884; those of *The Modern Regime* in 1891 and 1894.

1878 Taine is elected to the French Academy upon his third attempt.

1882 *Philosophy of Art,* the collected writings from Taine's lectures on art in Italy, the Netherlands, and Greece, as well as on the ideal in art, published separately between 1865

and 1869.
1885 In bad health, Taine has to interrupt his work.
1891 Article on "The Church" appears in *Revue des Deux Mondes*.
1892 Articles on "The School" in *Revue des Deux Mondes*. Taine falls seriously ill.
1893 Death of Taine, March 5.
1894 *Last Critical and Historical Essays* are published posthumously.

CHAPTER 1

The Man and His Times

How much does one have to know about the life of a great thinker to understand his works? If we consulted Hippolyte Taine himself, the answer would be: very little, even in the case of a writer of fiction. All that is required, it would seem, is to find the main spring that makes him tick, and all the rest can be deduced from this principal factor.

"A soul," he claims, "has its mechanism the same way as a plant: it belongs in the realm of science, and once we know the power at its source, we could, even without taking its works apart, reconstruct it by pure reasoning."[1] "Forty books are more than sufficient to know a man."[2]

I *The Intellectual Atmosphere*

Even though he probably had very little to hide (or, at any rate, not more than the average person),[3] Taine went to unusual pains to have his privacy protected during his lifetime and even after his death. In his last will he stipulated: "The only letters that may be published are those dealing with purely general or speculative matters, such as philosophy, history, esthetics, art, psychology; even in these, any passages that touch directly or indirectly on private affairs should be omitted, and no letter may be published without the authorization of my heirs and only once the above-mentioned cuts have been made by them."[4]

This request was scrupulously observed by the editors of his published notes and letters.[5] Still, in spite of the heavy editing, an image of the man comes through and it is of course favorable. Families have an understandable tendency to canonize their great men, especially if they have been called saints.[6] We may be sure that unfavorable material, if any, has been carefully excised. Be that as it may, there is much evidence to indicate that Taine was kind and courteous, fair-minded, loyal to his friends, ready to help any writer in whom he saw talent, and a splendid family man intensely concerned with the material and spiritual well-being of his wife and two children. These are admirable traits, but they do not provide much help to the understanding of his works.

Let us try another approach, his own, by looking for that master faculty which is to supply us with the key to all we need to know. If we consult Taine's friends and critics, the result is total confusion. "The thought of Spinoza projected through the imagination of Shakespeare,"[7] "the power of abstraction,"[8] "logical power,"[9] "the Don Juan of knowledge,"[10] "a poet-logician,"[11] these are some of the definitions proposed. Do they all define the same man?

Even if there is no general agreement on Taine's master faculty, one fact is beyond dispute: that he was an important thinker, one who, along with Ernest Renan, dominated intellectual life in France for a quarter of a century, during the period from about 1865 to his death in 1893.

By the middle of the nineteenth century, Romanticism had run its course in France and a new era was commencing. It was no longer a time for flights of fancy which had inspired the lyrical poetry of long-maned writers. A powerful force was finally asserting its full influence: science, deaf to unsubstantiated theories and blind to unobservable spiritual entities, interested only in facts, evidence, experimentation, and measurements.

Important advances, particularly in physiology and medicine, had raised immense hopes that science might soon solve all important problems and jubilant predictions were contained in Ernest Renan's *The Future of Science*.[12] As late as 1885 Berthelot proclaimed triumphantly that "today the world is without mystery."[13] In the 1860's the French translation of Darwin's *Origin of Species* was beginning to make its impact felt, but probably the most important work in popularizing science and its method was Claude Bernard's *Introduction to Experimental Medicine* (1865).[14]

With increasing prosperity a materialistic attitude put an end to adventurous but self-indulgent Romanticism.[15] Why could scientific methods not be applied to the solution of moral and social problems? Why not, for that matter, to literature and art where intuition and that indefinable quality called taste were still reigning supreme? Philosophy, too, soon felt the impact of this new trend as Auguste Comte propounded the sober ideas of positivism in opposition to the vague spiritual philosophy known as eclecticism which Victor Cousin had so eloquently presented in his lectures at the Sorbonne. While disagreeing with both of these, Taine attacked especially eclecticism with his ironic hammerblows, by exposing it to the unmerciful examination of scientific proof.[16]

Anatole France, by no means an uncritical admirer of Taine, rendered him this homage: "The thought of this powerful mind inspired in us, about 1870, an ardent enthusiasm, a sort of religion, I would call it the dynamic cult of life. What he offered us was the method of observation, the notion of fact and of idea, philosophy, history; at last here was science. And he unburdened us of that odious academic spiritualism."[17] "No one since Hegel perhaps," adds F. Brunetière, "has put into circulation more new and profound ideas about the history of literature and art, perhaps true, perhaps false, but at any rate *suggestive* and *provocative,* than the author of the *Philosophy of Art.*"[18]

It will be necessary to take a close look at the life of this man, for he was, like most human beings, a web of contradictions some of which may explain his views, his strengths, and his shortcomings.

II   *Taine's Life*

Hippolyte-Adolphe Taine was born on April 21, 1828 at Vouziers in the Ardennes mountains. His family, of modest middle class, had lived in that region since 1675. His great-grandfather had been nicknamed "the Philosopher." His father, a country lawyer, died in 1840 and young Hippolyte was sent to Paris where he studied at a boarding school while also attending classes at the Bourbon College. He was soon joined in Paris by his mother, whom he loved deeply, and his two sisters.

At the age of twenty, while preparing himself for admission to the Ecole Normale, Taine expressed the anguish caused by his loss of religious faith in the treatise "Of Human Destiny." This is one of the very few published documents in which the author speaks freely, enabling us thereby to understand his inner life during those important years of intellectual and emotional formation:

> Until the age of fifteen I lived in ignorance and tranquility. I had not yet thought of the future; I knew nothing of it; I was a Christian, and I had never asked myself what this life is worth, where I came from, and what I had to do. . . . Reason appeared in me like a beacon light. I began to suspect that there was something beyond what I had seen, and to grope as in darkness. My religious faith was the first thing which fell before this spirit of inquiry. One doubt provoked another; each article of disbelief dragged another down with it in its fall. . . .

> The three following years were happy, three years of research and discovery. I thought but of enlarging my intelligence, increasing my knowledge, and acquiring a stronger sentiment of Truth and of the Beautiful. I ardently studied History and Antiquity, ever seeking for general truths, aspiring to the knowledge of the whole, i.e. of Man and of Society. . . .

> I placed my mind at the service of the newest and most poetical opinion, I supported Pantheism with all my heart. I affected to speak as an artist; this new world pleased me, and I amused myself by exploring it in all its parts. This was my salvation, for, from that moment, metaphysics appeared to me intelligible, and science seemed serious. I reached, after much effort, a height from which I could embrace the whole of the philosophical horizon, understand the opposition of systems, see the birth of opinions, discover the knot of divergences and the solution of difficulties. I learnt what to examine in order to find out what was fallacious and what was true. I saw the point towards which my researches should tend. Moreover, I was already in possession of Method, which I had studied from curiosity, and for my own amusement. Henceforth I ardently set to work; the clouds dispersed, I understood the origin of my errors, I perceived the Whole and the connecting links.[19]

He began his studies at the Ecole Normale Supérieure[20] in 1848 at the head of a brilliant class which included Edmond About, Francisque Sarcey, Edouard de Suckau and, a year later, his close friend Anatole Prévost-Paradol.[21] Although unhappy at first, Taine quickly rose to the role of president of his section. He later looked back on these years of study as the most fruitful of his life. Indeed, it was there that he read voraciously. Like his fellow students, he admired the literary criticisms of Sainte-Beuve, and, most important of all, under the guidance of a young professor, Paul

Jacquinet, he discovered the author he was to prefer above all others: Stendhal. There too he devoured the works of Hegel and Kant, but especially of Spinoza, who was to cause his downfall in the examinations for the *agrégation* in 1851. The conservative board of examiners found his lesson on Spinoza's moral system absurd, and thus, as both teachers and students listened in disbelief, the most brilliant candidate of the class was declared to have failed.

Taine took this disappointment philosophically and decided to accept an assignment as substitute teacher at the College of Nevers. Despite mediocre students and loneliness, he continued his own work at first in the hope of writing a dissertation on psychology and, when this project was refused, he prepared a doctorate in literature.

A severe crisis arose when professors were asked to sign a loyalty oath in favor of Louis Napoleon who had just carried out his successful coup d'état. This oath read: "We the undersigned declare our adherence to the measures taken by the President of the Republic on December 2 [1851], and offer him the expression of our gratitude and our respectful devotion." Taine refused to sign, a gesture that may be interpreted as a rebellious attitude; however, his refusal represents rather an unwillingness to recognize a government that came to power by illegitimate means. Once Louis-Bonaparte was properly elected, Taine did not see any objection to signing a statement of adherence, much to the despair of his ultra-liberal friend Prévost-Paradol. Yet the Minister of Education continued to look askance on the unorthodox philosophical views of the young scholar, and after a brief appointment at Poitiers, Taine was demoted to teaching sixth grade at Besançon in 1852.

Rather than accept this humiliation, he asked for a leave of absence in order to return to Paris where he eked out a living by giving private lessons supplemented by a modest income of his own. Taine was not to return to teaching until 1864; instead he prepared his dissertation on a subject to which no objections could be raised: the *Fables* of La Fontaine, which earned him his doctorate in 1853. A cure in the Pyrenees mountains occasioned the first of several travel books[22] for Hachette who was to become his publisher. Collaboration on several reviews[23] enabled him to gain experience in literary criticism. He also completed his scientific education through courses at the Faculty of Medicine, the Sorbonne, and the mental hospital of La Salpêtrière in Paris. Until 1857 he continued his study of physiology and natural sciences by attending the lectures of famous professors, including those of Isodore Geoffroy Saint-Hilaire, and by extensive reading.

Nevertheless, the young scholar continued to be viewed with much distrust by the authorities. His *Essay on Livy* which he submitted for a competition to the French Academy in 1854 disturbed the venerable forty "immortals" so much that they decided to give no award that year. Only after certain objectionable passages[24] had been changed did he receive the prize the following year. By 1864, when Taine submitted the first three volumes of his *History of English Literature,* the French Academy had not changed its attitude toward this man with radical philosophical views. Again no prize was awarded that year, and so, contrary to the *Essay on Livy,* the *History of English Literature,* by far the more important of the two works, received no recognition from the French Academy. Even a minor post as admissions examiner at the Military Academy of Saint-Cyr in 1863 met with a good deal of opposition and his appointment as professor at the Ecole des Beaux-Arts in 1864 scandalized conservative academicians.

It is true that Taine had done little to gain the sympathy of those men who dominated French intellectual life around midcentury. His interest in Hegel and Spinoza had led to his failure in the examinations for the *agrégation,* his proposed dissertation on psychology had been declared unacceptable, but, most of all, his attack on the reigning philosophers of the day had been deeply resented by Victor Cousin and his large following. Although Taine was bound to oppose these thinkers on philosophical grounds, the biting, ironic tone in *The Nineteenth Century Classical Philosophers* goes beyond academic criticism and reflects the personal resentment which past encounters with representatives of this group had aroused in him.

On the other hand, his attacks on authority gained him the enthusiastic support of the students. Those at the Ecole des Beaux-Arts had hooted Viollet-le-Duc off the platform when he attempted to give his first lectures. Taine, named his successor, was greeted with an ovation. Witnesses have immortalized that scene:

The audience, seated in a huge semi-circular hall, faces the professor who . . . resembles a Protestant minister in his pulpit, bearded, wearing glasses and speaking simply to men like himself. The students are more attentive than one would expect from these young bearded and long-haired men with their bright eyes and mocking expressions. The professor seems as young as his students. . . . He is dressed in black, his coat buttoned up. On the table his hat, his gloves, a few sheets of penciled notes.[25]

The teacher was speaking in his somewhat monotonous voice, his accent sounded vaguely foreign. . . . This man, so modest that he seemed unaware of his European reputation and so simple that his only concern seemed to be to serve truth, became for us the apostle of a New Faith. Here was a man who had never sacrificed on the altar of official doctrines, this man had never lied.[26]

In the midst of all these activities Taine found time to begin a novel, *Etienne Mayran,* which he abandoned after having written eighty pages because, applying his critical acumen to his own work, he found it was merely personal psychological analysis. He also led an active social life, being received in various literary salons, including those of Mme. Guizot and the Princess Mathilde and taking part in the famous dinners at the Restaurant Magny, presided over by Sainte-Beuve, in the company of Théophile Gautier, Gustave Flaubert, George Sand, Turgenev and the brothers Goncourt. The nasty descriptions in the notes taken by the latter made him gradually neglect these literary gatherings. No doubt his marriage in 1868 with the daughter of an architect and patron of the arts constituted an important turning point in his life.

In 1870 Taine completed one of his most cherished projects: *On Intelligence,* the treatise on psychology he had contemplated writing for over twenty years and which placed him in the forefront in that field along with Wundt. "The book will be read by a hundred people in France and by about as many in the rest of Europe," he said at the time of its publication. Yet such was the success of this difficult work that 12,000 copies had been sold by 1903.

The year 1870 was an eventful one for Taine in other ways as well. In June he had left on a trip to Germany with the purpose of writing a work on German literature, but the death of his mother-in-law obliged him to return to France on July 12. The subsequent Franco-Prussian War awakened in him an intense patriotism which made him abandon the projected work on Germany. At the same time the uprising of the Paris Commune in 1871 and a first hand observation of a popular revolt left a lasting impression on Taine, no doubt deepening an already latent political conservatism.

As early as 1849[27] the twenty-one-year-old Taine had stated his two basic political beliefs: (1) that the right to acquire, own, and dispose of property is absolute, and (2) that all political rights of the citizen come down to a single one: the right to give his consent, explicitly or tacitly, to the existing government, so that the type of government in itself is of no importance since it derives its legitimacy only from the acceptance of the nation.

Consequently "the most acceptable government is one directed by the most capable and most honest people, that is to say, the upper classes, the bourgeoisie and nobility. If these upper classes are mediocre and even stupid, that is annoying, but we have nothing better."[28] On the other hand, he maintained that the greatest danger to freedom is a centralized government and that its functions should be limited to that of a gendarme against robbers at home and enemies abroad.[29]

Opposed both to women's suffrage and universal suffrage, Taine saw his ideal government in Protestant England and his ideal man in the English aristocrat. For him "the man of high standing is the man of leisure, who has no trade, who is concerned with broad views, who takes the lead, like the English aristocracy of our own days, or the Roman and Greek of other times. If this aristocracy is to endure and conciliate, it must devote its strength and its time to the public service."[30]

Thus, while the Commune of 1871 contributed substantially to confirm his distrust of popular government, it would be incorrect to claim that this experience did more than reinforce the political views he had developed over a long period of time and which we find prominently expressed in the work which occupied him during the last twenty years of his life: *The Origins of Contemporary France,* on which he began research in 1872.

Prior to that he had accepted an invitation to lecture on Corneille and Racine at Oxford University where he received an honorary doctor's degree. Even the French Academy finally recognized his merit by electing him to membership in 1878 after two unsuccessful attempts. By that time his material life had changed considerably. In 1874 Taine bought a country home at Menthon-Saint-Bernard (Savoie) near the Lake of Annecy, where he lived most of the year except for a few months in the winter which he spent in Paris. There, on Mondays, at the rue Cassette, the Taines used to receive about fifteen guests for dinner. Among the "habitués" we find many of Taine's closest friends: Paul Bourget, Melchior de Vogüé, Ernest Renan, Gaston Paris, José-Maria de Hérédia, the brothers Berthelot, and Ernest Lavisse.[31]

Feeling that France was in serious trouble, Taine turned to a historical study: *The Origins of Contemporary France.* As early as 1849 he had stated: "In order to vote, I should have to know the condition of France, its ideas, manners and customs, opinions, and future, for the true government is that which is appropriate to the civilization of the people."[32] The experience of the Commune uprising in 1871 and subsequent political events in France moved him to study his country and its recent history the way a doctor would examine a very sick patient.

As each of the volumes came off the press it was greeted with reactions divided along party lines. By the time the work neared its end Taine had incurred the disfavor of all political groups of his time. The *Ancien Régime,* which criticized the injustices and errors of royal governments from Louis XIV to the Revolution, angered conservatives and royalists and gained him the applause of liberals. The volumes dealing with the Revolution completely reversed these attitudes. The author was violently attacked by liberal politicians and historians. More than that, he had dared to stigmatize an epoch that was viewed with almost religious awe by many Frenchmen. Finally Taine took on another idol: Napoleon. This time he took greater precautions, for he valued his cordial relations with the Princess Mathilde, Napoleon's niece. He had informed her of his project and received her approval of his summary: "My conclusion about the Emperor is this: the greatest genius of modern times, an egoism equal to his genius."[33] But when the Princess read the full text, she used a casual reference to her grandmother's having been parsimonious and indifferent to cleanliness as a pretext to break with Taine. This loss of an esteemed friendship hurt the historian more than all the bitter attacks from various political quarters. Pursued by worsening health

Taine still managed to publish an article on the Church in 1891 and another one on the school system in 1892. After much suffering he died on March 5, 1893. He is buried near his country home in Savoy, on the hill which overlooks Boringe at Menthon-Saint-Bernard.

III   *Taine's Character and Beliefs*

There is a good deal of evidence that Taine was buried not as a Catholic but rather as a Protestant, if not a converted one then at least closer to Protestantism than any other religion. Although a believer in God, Taine had been persistently anticlerical, writing as late as 1891: "As for religion, what seems to me incompatible with modern science, is not Christianity but present-day Roman Catholicism; by contrast, science may be reconciled with broad-minded and liberal Protestantism."[34]

In his last years he expressed a somewhat more favorable attitude toward the Catholic Church, seeing in it a bulwark, a sort of spiritual gendarme, against social chaos; nevertheless, he had his children raised in the liberal Protestant faith. At his deathbed was Pastor H. Hollard who also pronounced the funeral oration. A previous attempt by Monsignor d'Hulst to convert Taine back to Catholicism had been unsuccessful.

Taine did not quite complete his last work. He had intended to conclude his vast survey of modern France with studies on *Association* and *The Family* to be followed by a last volume on the *Modern Regime.* His life too was not quite complete, for, more than unpublished correspondence, what is lacking is a final stand that would have given us the full measure of the man. Taine died before the Dreyfus Affair forced Frenchmen to take sides. The majority of Taine's friends were strongly conservative. He had joined an anti-socialist league in 1891 and Charles Maurras, the ultra-conservative editor of *L'Action Française,* was to praise Taine for his political views in several articles. If he were to be judged by those writers who felt his influence so strongly that they depicted him in a novel,[35] one could only conclude that he would have placed the preservation of social order above the need of according fair justice to an individual.

But Taine also had liberal friends, among them Prévost-Paradol, the man closest to his heart during his youth, and Ernest Renan.

Moreover, he had repeatedly stated his preference for the English governmental system and he had praised the United States for its policy of separating Church and State.[36]

It is impossible to conjecture with any certainty with which side Taine would have aligned himself, for he was far from predictable, as those who tried to derive political profit from his historical writings found out to their sorrow. But let us turn from speculations about his political beliefs to those traits and opinions of Taine that may have influenced his writings.

In attempting to assess the works of an author such as Taine who claimed to have applied scientific methods to the study of philosophy, literature, art, psychology, and history, it is necessary to look for any peculiar propensities that may have prevented him from being as objective as his method requires. A mere examination of his style and his literary preferences reveal that Taine was not the cold calculating machine that some of his critics saw in him. "Taine is a writer," H. F. Amiel complains, "whose work always produces a disagreeable impression on me, as though of creaking of pulleys and clicking of machinery. There is a smell of laboratory about it. His style is a style of chemistry and technology. The science of it is inexorable; it is dry and forcible, penetrating and hard, strong and harsh, but altogether lacking in charm, humanity, nobility, and grace."[37]

In spite of a cold exterior appearance, Taine was a man of deep passions, likes and dislikes. Persistent and undaunted as those strong trees in his native Ardennes forests he loved so much, he carried on with his work regardless of the harm he was doing to his health. But his state of mind was by no means uniform. In 1862, at the time he was undertaking his first major work, *The History of English Literature,* he took stock in two highly revealing personal notes. The first is optimistic:

My turn of mind is French and Latin, classing ideas in regular and progressive lines in the manner of the natural scientists, according to the rules of the Ideologists, in short, oratorically. . . . My effort is to reach the essence, as the Germans say, not by scaling the rock but by a smooth usable road. To replace intuition (insight) and sudden abstraction (Geist, Vernunft) by oratorical analysis. . . . For the past ten years all the currents of my reflections and education have been tending to transform the dry, abstract ideas into developed and living ones. It is the passage from formula to life; what was formerly the skeleton has taken on flesh.[38]

But only eight months later he arrived at some very disturbing conclusions:

When I look within myself, it seems to me that my state of mind has changed, that I have destroyed within me my oratorical and rhetorical talents. My ideas no longer fall into ranks as they used to, I am traversed by ideas that come like lightning, vehement sensations. impulses, words, images; in short, my state of mind is rather that of an artist than that of a writer. I struggle between these two tendencies, the former and the present one. . . . As a result I try very hard but do not always succeed. Besides. when I attain the proper state of mind, it only lasts an hour or half an hour; at any rate, it is killing me. I have probably attempted to join two irreconcilable faculties. I must choose: to be an artist or an oratorical writer.[39]

The man who bitterly satirized the fashionable French philosophers of his youth, who grew ecstatic in nature, who adored the Italian Renaissance, who found consolation in the works of Marcus Aurelius, who preferred Shakespeare, Goethe, Byron, Balzac, Stendhal, and Musset in literature, even though he was highly critical of the French Romantics, shared their hostility toward the Classical seventeenth and eighteenth centuries and Racine in particular, and who covered the French revolutionaries with most unobjective invectives, this man was consumed by an inner flame that was kept from exploding only by a purposely cold scientific method. In fact, one of the questions that will have to be considered is whether Taine, in spite of his enormous knowledge, a man ideally prepared for interdisciplinary studies, was temperamentally suited to carry out his work with maximum results.

It should be obvious by now that no simple formula can summarize Taine as a person or expose his master faculty. Even those who were close to him did not always judge him very accurately. Thus the Danish critic Georges Brandès sees two discordant persons in Taine, the writer and the man: "As an intellect, he was a Renaissance man, lacking in flexibility, but daring, rich, fond of grandiose and passionate strength; besides, a poet unafraid of sickly or putrid aspects so important in modern poetry, a devoted admirer of Alfred de Musset and Heinrich Heine. As a private man, on the contrary, extremely bourgeois (a settled-down academician) who never had left the straight and narrow path nor committed an act that would attract public attention. He looked with a sort of amazed pity upon those who let themselves be engulfed in their daily life by their lyrical aspirations."[40] Brandès might have added that, in private life, Taine was also an alarmist, seeing disaster descending upon the unstable French governmental structure at any moment, but it is the thinker, the writer, who has far outlived the bearded, bespectacled individual.

CHAPTER 2

Philosophy, Method, and Psychology

A man of many talents turns easily into a dilettante. There was no such danger for Taine, one of the last modern men of universal knowledge and achievements. But among so many fields of endeavor, one no doubt predominated. Was he primarily a philosopher? a critic of literature and art? a psychologist or an historian?

His own answer would have assigned the first place to psychology. "All I have been doing for the past forty years," he wrote in 1891, "has been applied or pure psychology."[1] Consequently his key work would be *On Intelligence,* his treatise on psychology. If this were to be our conclusion today, little would be left to say about Taine, for his psychology, however important it may have been in 1870, has been ant-eaten (or rather Freud-eaten) and the entire edifice of his tightly constructed method would come tumbling down.

I *The Philosophical Background*

No doubt, psychology was dearest to Taine's heart and he came to literature and art almost by accident; yet paradoxically, his most lasting contributions are in these fields. By elimination we are left with a choice between philosophy and history. A number of critics hold that he was first of all a philosopher, but his relatively small philosophical output would militate against that view.[2] Thus we are led to conclude that Taine was above all an historian, but an historian of a special kind. To begin with, he was a philosophical historian, i.e. one not concerned particularly with the recital of dates and battles and facts per se but with the causes behind those facts; furthermore, he attempted to characterize the spirit of the period he was examining, and this attitude places him among the pioneers of studies in the history of ideas; finally, he used the tools of psychology to penetrate as deeply as possible into the minds of the individuals he was portraying. To apply Taine's method of summing up a master faculty in a brief phrase, we may define him as a philosophical historian who sought the psychological factors behind people and events.[3]

In dealing with Taine the philosopher it matters therefore far less to establish his brand of philosophy[4] nor, for the purposes of this study at least, to trace in detail the influences which shaped his thought,[5] than to set forth his method and those philosophical attitudes and assumptions on which it was based. For Taine was not an original philosopher. He drew heavily on Aristotle, Spinoza, Hegel, Stuart Mill and others, and he freely admitted his borrowings.

The philosopher to whom he gave least credit, perhaps because of his general dislike of the seventeenth-century rational spirit, was Descartes; yet, in many ways Taine was continuing in the nineteenth century an effort begun by the man who is generally considered the father of modern philosophy. At least three basic attitudes are common to both Descartes and Taine: (1) to rid philosophy of scholastic and spiritual entities; (2) to proceed in an orderly step-by-step method based on factual evidence; (3) to apply to moral subject matter the processes and tools provided by the state of science at the time. In the seventeenth century, the greatest progress in science had been made by mathematics, so Descartes relied heavily on that field for his method; in Taine's time the physical and natural sciences had moved ahead.[6] But Taine was not satisfied merely to bring Descartes up-to-date. Where his predecessor had essentially exposed a method and indicated what could be done with it, Taine's great vision consisted in applying his own method boldly to literature, art, psychology, and history.

Taine had formed his basic philosophical attitudes during his studies at the Ecole Normale (1848-1851) where he read extensively, adopting Aristotle and especially Spinoza as his masters. As early as 1849 he realized that method would have to be his greatest concern: "Everything depends on the method; so I come back to that subject. By method I mean the means of having true perceptions, in other words, the necessary conditions for having a series of true perceptions. By the truth of a perception I mean its agreeing with its object; I mean it should be subjectively what the object is in itself."[7]

II *Attack on the Reigning Philosophers*

The young philosopher found sympathy among his teachers who thought very highly of him, but official attitudes remained hostile to his views which were largely responsible for his failure in the examination for the *agrégation* in 1851. He realized then that he would first have to overthrow the reigning philosophy of the day, represented by Victor Cousin, Pierre-Paul Royer-Collard, Maine de Biran and Théodore Jouffroy and variously called eclecticism or spiritualism. But he also refused to espouse opposing ideas of positivism represented in France by Auguste Comte. Although far more sympathetic to the latter view, he found himself obliged to fight both these philosophical schools.

Taine's *The Nineteenth Century Classical Philosophers* (1857)[8] is his most exuberant work, full of youthful vigor and a mocking, satirical tone worthy of Voltaire. Taine examined the works of the eclectic philosophers for their meaning and found them wanting in clarity, in facts, and in criteria that could resist a scientific scrutiny. Today only Maine de Biran enjoys still some repute (and Taine's criticism of him was neither always fair nor convincing), so it would serve little purpose to expose Taine's attacks on each one in detail. However, one of the most entertaining passages will demonstrate the approach used by Taine. He pretends he is discussing Maine de Biran's work with a young medical student who claims that everything in it is gibberish. Whereupon Taine proceeds to prove that, even though Maine de Biran may at times be wrong or superficial, one can understand his lucubrations by translating them into simple language:

I return to your last sentence. Permit me to copy it in its entirety: "Every one can observe in himself that the direct perceptions of the external senses, as the images or intuitions of the internal sense, and the very ideas, products elaborated by our intelligence, coming to be reflected upon or contemplated successively by the self under diverse sensitive modifications or with a variable sentiment of existence, sad or painful, pleasant or easy, etc., are proportionate up to a certain point to these variations, as for the degree of clarity or obscurity, mobility

or persistence, trustworthiness or doubt, which imprint on these ideas
a particular aspect, something like a physiognomy of its own."

This phrase would have frightened Hegel or Duns Scotus himself.
And yet, after reading the entire passage, one finds that it contains a
very simple and very true meaning, namely: "When you have diarrhea
or a migraine headache, your reasoning is less clear, your attention less
lasting, your conclusions less sure than when you are in good health."[9]

Probing for the causes of the shortcomings of eclectic philosophy, Taine finds two: (1) the need of subordinating science to
morality; (2) the predilection for abstract words.

This preference for morality finally reshaped M. Cousin's entire
philosophy. Thus transformed he refuted skepticism, an immoral doctrine, by an equivocation, reduced psychology to the study of reason
and freedom, the only faculties related to morality, defined reason and
freedom in a way that would serve morality, set up God as guardian of
morality, and the immortality of the soul as sanction for morality. Thus
he suppressed philosophical philosophy, leaving old objections unan-
swered, repeating old demonstrations, obliterating questions of science,
and reducing science to an oratorical apparatus for the purposes of
education and government. . . .

This bent for abstraction[10] persuaded M. de Biran to transform
forces, simple qualities or abstract relationships, into substances, to
consider will as the soul, to change extension into an appearance and
to resuscitate Leibnitz's monads.

This bent for abstraction, after having led M. Cousin into pantheism,
reduced his philosophy to a heap of inaccurate phrases, of lame reason-
ings, and obvious equivocations; so that, when later his love for the
seventeenth century had taught him what a simple style is, his doctrines reposed only on public prejudice, on his glory as a philosopher
and on his genius as an orator.[11]

Finally Taine topped off his satirical attack by depicting the eclectic philosophers as being out of touch with their times: Victor
Cousin should have been a theologian, a fashionable preacher during the seventeenth century, distinguishing himself as an orator
and as a disciple of Bossuet. Jouffroy's real calling was to have
been born in England in 1680 as a Protestant and a disinterested
philosopher living in retirement.

III   *Cause, Analysis, and Synthesis*

Even though Taine's entertaining manner of heaping ridicule on the philosophy of the day created a sensation and made him well known overnight, it is not the critical side of the book that matters greatly today. We are far more interested in the positive sections of *The Nineteenth Century Classical Philosophers:* the preface and the concluding chapter entitled "On Method." In these few pages Taine exposes his own views which will remain the basis of his philosophical attitude.

Why will he accept neither spiritualism nor positivism? The principal reason is his disagreement with them on what is meant by cause. For the spiritualists, causes or forces are distinct beings outside of bodies and qualities of the senses; hence they believe that there exists an invisible, intangible world which produces the other one and sustains it. For them the cause of life is the life force, a distinct incorporeal entity. The positivists, on the other hand, consider causes or forces, especially first causes, as beyond human knowledge; hence they can neither affirm nor deny them. The cause of life cannot be known, we can only note the sum total and direction of chemical reactions and the physical action that constitutes life, and then group together the experimental laws which sum up all the observed facts in our universe. Thus causes are seen by the spiritualists as being outside of objects, and by the positivists as outside of science.

Taine refutes both these views by claiming that causes are generative facts, that the effect is implicitly contained in the cause, that the effect reveals the cause, that the cause implies the effect, that the two are basically the same thing expressed in different terms.[12] He assigns to science the task of finding the cause of each object and the cause of causes which is that of the universe.[13] This conception of cause, which Taine calls variously force or generative factor, is central to all his thought. The definition of cause to which Taine will always return is this: the cause of a fact is the law or the dominant quality from which it is deduced; a cause is a fact which, once known, enables us to deduce from it the nature, relationships and changes of the other dependent facts.[14]

What is needed therefore is a method of finding the cause by scrupulously sticking to facts. In the final chapters of *The Nineteenth Century Classical Philosophers* Taine exposes this method by introducing two philosophers: M. Pierre and M. Paul.

M. Pierre demonstrates the method of analysis. "To analyze

means to translate. . . . In this translation I see two steps. The first is exact translation, the kind Condillac explains; the second is complete translation."[15] The first step is illustrated by an analysis of the term "vital force." The term in itself is meaningless, so we have to translate. If we look at an animal's teeth, tongue, and other parts of the mouth, we realize they have to be as they are so that the animal can chew; the same holds true of the act of swallowing, digesting, briefly of all the bodily functions, all of which are necessary for the preservation of life. Life is the end; the operation of the body, the means. Thus we are dealing with a relationship, in this case the relationship between life and the bodily functions. Once we know this, we may speak metaphorically of a force in the organized body but we know that it is neither a quality nor a substance but a simple relationship.

"I no longer see any fluid, monad or mystery, but only two orders of facts: one principal fact, the process of destruction and renewal that is called life; subordinate facts: the functions and the structure that make these functions possible; a relationship is the necessity which attaches these subordinate facts to the principal fact. Facts, relationships, there is nothing other than these. We have purged our mind of a metaphysical being."[16]

The second step, complete translation, requires filling in the unknown parts by known quantities in the manner of algebra. This requires the use of instruments. The phrase "the animal digests" seems clear, yet it is only by means of the scalpel, the microscope and chemistry that the full meaning of this process can be known.

Analysis stops here; you know what it consists of: translating words by facts, that is its definition; exact translation, complete translation are its two parts. In exact translation, we turn obscure, vague, abstract words of complicated and doubtful meaning into the facts, into the portions of facts, into the relationship and combinations of facts that they mean. . . . In complete translation . . . we add to the knowledge of each noted fact the knowledge of the unknowns around it. To do this, we modify the object under observation or we replace the observing instrument. Once these two operations have been completed, I see nothing else left to be done.[17]

At this moment M. Paul takes over. He agrees with everything M. Pierre has said but insists his friend has not gone far enough.

Take an animal, a dog, a man, a raven, a carp; what is his essence or his cause? All the steps of the method are effects of that question.

After having classified the parts and the functions of their living body and considered for some time their relationships and successions, I extract a general fact, that is, one common to all the parts of the living body and to every moment of life: nutrition or repair of the organs. I assume that it is the cause of a group of other facts and I am going to verify this hypothesis. If the verification proves me wrong, I shall take one by one the general facts surrounding this one until by probing I shall hit upon those which are causes.[18]

M. Paul then proceeds to prove by verification that nutrition is a cause,[19] and that, likewise, destruction or continuous dissolution and type (i.e. animal, man, etc.) are causes. "Abstraction, hypothesis, verification; these are the three steps of the method."[20]

IV   The Application of Physical Laws to Human Affairs

So far Taine has exposed a method of investigation used in the sciences, such as Claude Bernard will present eight years later to the general public in his well-known Introduction to the Study of Experimental Medicine (1865). We gather as many facts as possible, classify them, find out what their necessary relationships are, establish a hypothesis of experimental laws on the basis of the observed cases, transform the multitude of diverse actions into a hierarchy of causes and, if possible, go on from there to set up some generative and universal axiom.

Had Taine stopped there, he would have been no more than a philosophical Claude Bernard. What makes him one of the most original thinkers of the nineteenth century is his idea that the method used in the physical sciences can be applied to moral subject matter as well. Or, in his own famous phrase: "Moral matters, as physical matters, have dependencies and conditions."[21] This implies, of course, a particular conception of man as being "not an assembly of contiguous pieces but a machine with well-ordered wheelworks: he is a system and not an accidental heap."[22] While Taine will not go anywhere as far as La Mettrie in speaking of Man the Machine,[23] he is an unswerving believer in determinism. From his preface to the Essay on Livy where he states categorically "Man, says Spinoza, is not in nature 'as an empire within an empire' but as part of a whole; and the movements of that spiritual automaton which is our being are as regulated as those of the material world in which he is included,"[24] to the striking formula which was to be continually misinterpreted ("Vice and virtue are products, like vitriol and sugar"),[25] Taine adhered to the principle that man's actions are determined by definite causes and that his freedom is limited at best. Once we thoroughly know the chain of events that determine our fate, we may be able to undo or alter one of the links of this chain and thereby influence all the following ones. This is the only concession he will make.

In general, the laws of the natural sciences apply to human affairs as well. In his constant search for unity and causes Taine was bound to be particularly attracted by those scientific laws which bore out his basic philosophical views. Cuvier's theory of the correlation of parts in organisms[26] which states that if one of the organisms changes, all the others will change accordingly, implies that the same dependence exists among the various aptitudes and inclinations of an individual, a race, or an epoch. The law of the subordination of characters in botany and zoology to the effect that some characteristics of an animal or vegetable group are preponderant and determine its structure while others are subordinated and variable, leads to his concept of the master faculty in a human group or individual. A consequence of this rule is Geoffroy Saint-Hilaire's theory of organic balance, namely, that the excessive development of one organ leads to a weakening of the corresponding organs. Thus Taine will explain the relative weakness of painting in Germany by an excessive attachment to abstract thinking which prevents realistic observation. The principle of analogy and unity of composition, proposed by Geoffroy Saint-Hilaire and developed by Richard Owen, that in a class or even an entire branch of the animal kingdom the same pattern of organization can be found in all its species is applied by Taine to prove that, in spite of modifications due to exterior circumstances, constant traits can be observed in a nation or a race. Finally Darwin's rule of natural selection holds true for humans as well, for those who succeed and survive possess the aptitudes and inclinations that correspond most closely to those of their group. Consequently, the greatest artists and writers are the most reliable and representative witnesses of their times.

Taine goes still further. This transference of physical laws to human affairs is not only limited to individuals but holds true as well of a race or an entire epoch. Speaking of the age of Louis XIV, he claims:

Between a bower in the garden of Versailles, a philosophical or theological argument of Malebranche, a rule of versification by Boileau, a law on mortgages by Colbert, an idle compliment at Marly, a phrase by Bossuet about the royalty of God, the distance seems infinite and unbridgeable; there seems to be no possible link. The facts are so dissimilar that, at first view, we judge them the way they appear, i.e. isolated and separate. But *the facts communicate amongst themselves by the definitions of the groups in which they are included.* . . . Each one is an action of that ideal and general man around whom all inventions and peculiarities of the period are gathered; each one has as its cause some aptitude or inclination of the reigning model. The various inclinations or aptitudes of this central character match, check and balance each other due to some propensity or dominating faculty, because the same mind and the same heart thought, prayed, imagined and acted, because the separate and diverse works have been fashioned and determined by the same general situation and the same inborn disposition, because the same seal has been stamped differently on different matters. None of these imprints can change without producing changes in the others, because if one of them changes, it can do so only by a change in the seal.[27]

Naturally these views created a sensation and Taine was angrily attacked by every partisan of human freedom and morality. This was to be expected and such Tainian slogans as "Man is a theorem that walks"[27a] were not likely to gain him many new friends. His comments and explanations are not always quite consistent, but he generally specified that laws concerning human affairs cannot be expressed in exact measurements, that hence he never intended to equate human affairs and geometry and, finally, that being a determinist does not exclude irreproachable moral conduct and judgment.

"I have never claimed," he wrote to his former professor Ernest Havet, "that in history and in the moral sciences theorems analogous to geometry may be applied; history is not a science analogous to geometry but to physiology and geology. Just as there are fixed but non-measurable relationships between the organs and the functions of a living body so there are exact relationships that, however, cannot be expressed numerically, between the groups of facts that make up social and moral life."[28]

"But though the means of notation are not the same in the moral and physical sciences, yet, as in both the pattern is the same, equally made up of forces, magnitudes and directions, we may say that in both the final result is produced after the same method. It is big or small, and as the fundamental forces are big or small and act more or less exactly in the same sense, according as the distinct effects of race, circumstance, and epoch combine to add the one to the other, or to annul one another."[29]

Two problems arise necessarily from this attitude. If man's conduct is governed by definite laws, can we praise or condemn his actions? Moreover, can a person be held responsible for what he does?

To the first question, Taine gives two different answers. One may indeed judge an individual of historical importance. "There is one standard by which philosophers and scholars should be judged; there is another one for writers, poets, painters, artists. There is a third standard for determining the worth of men of politics and practical action; the test is this: has the man in question tried and succeeded in diminishing or at least in not increasing the present and future sum total of human suffering?"[30] On the other hand, what interests him most in studying a historical or literary personage are the causes for his actions rather than their quality:

What matters it if Peter or Paul is a rascal? that is the business of his contemporaries: they suffered from his vices, and ought to think only of despising and condemning him. Now we are beyond his reach, and hatred has disappeared with the danger. At this distance, and in the historic perspective, I see in him but a mental machine, provided with certain springs, animated by a primary impulse, affected by various circumstances. I calculate the play of his motives; I feel with him the impact of obstacles; I see beforehand the curve which his motion will trace out; I experience for him neither aversion nor disgust; I have left these feelings on the threshold of history, and I taste the very deep and pure pleasure of seeing a soul act after a definite law, in a fixed groove, with all the variety of human passions, with the succession and constraint which the inner structure of man imposes on the external development of his passions.[31]

To the second question Taine replied affirmatively. Pointing to the long list of his predecessors, he was able to maintain that determinism and moral responsibility are not only compatible but usually found together. "The most rigid and convinced moralists have been necessitarian determinists, not only Spinoza, Leibnitz and other great isolated minds but practicing sects: the stoics for five hundred years, the Calvinists and the Puritans since the Reformation."[32]

V *Illustrations of Taine's Method*

It is not enough to have a method; it has to be applied. At first view this would require an exceptionally educated and gifted person. However, his nephew, André Chevrillon, reports that such was not Taine's opinion: "This method . . . had, according to him, the advantage of not requiring any genius, and to the objection that the analysis involved might be a random one or would not come to a correct conclusion if not guided by a prerequisite, intuitive view that not just anybody is capable of, he replied: 'No, the idea springs forth from the examination of the facts, one soon sees them shaping into groups and one quickly distinguishes the principal ones. All it takes is a certain critical education and some experience in this type of study.' "[33]

As usual, Taine was not simply engaging in the game of startling statements. He was prepared to prove his point by exposing a recipe for use by prospective critics who could satisfy the minimum requirements:

The reader will take some artist, scholar, or important writer, a given poet or novelist, and read his works, pen in hand. In order to read them well, he will divide them into natural groups, and in each group he will take note of those three distinct features that are called personages or characters, action or plot, style or manner of writing. In each of these divisions, he will indicate in a few brief and vivid words, according to the habitual manner used by critics, the striking peculiarities, the dominant traits and the characteristic qualities of the author. At the end of this first phase, if he has had some practice in this sort of work, an involuntary phrase, unusually strong and significant, will spring forth from his pen which will sum up his entire examination and expose to him a certain type of taste and talent, a certain disposition of mind and soul, a certain procession of likes and dislikes, of strengths and weaknesses, in short, a certain *psychological state* which dominates and persists: that of the author.

Let him now repeat the same operation on the other parts of the same subject; next. let him compare the three or four summaries which have resulted from each of these partial analyses; now let him add to the writings the life of the author, I mean his conduct with people, his philosophy, that is, his way of looking at the world, his ethics and his esthetics, that is, his concerted views about what is good and what is beautiful; finally, let him compare and reconcile all the brief phrases which are the concentrated essence of the thousands of remarks and the hundreds of judgments he has made. If his notations are accurate, if he has acquired the habit of perceiving the feelings and the faculties beneath the words that denote them, if he is sufficiently endowed with that interior eye by means of which we define instantly the diverse aspects of the spiritual being, he will see that the seven or eight formulas *depend* on one another, that, once the first was given, the others could not be different, that consequently the qualities they represent are linked, that if one were to vary, the others would vary proportionally, and that therefore they form a system as an organized body.[34]

This example applies to a relatively simple case: that of studying an individual author. As it turns out, even that operation requires far more than an ordinary reader. As the subject increases in complexity, the burden of research becomes of course proportionally heavier, yet the basic procedure remains the same. Let us assume we wish to examine an entire period or even the history of a people. We still have to classify facts in natural groups, but these groups will now be different. First come the three great works of human intelligence: religion, art, and philosophy; next the two great works of human association: the family and the State; finally the three great material works of human labor: industry, commerce, and agriculture. Each of these major groups will, in turn, have its subdivisions. Once more a comparison of the characteristics observed, if properly noted, will show that all these groups possess in common certain generative factors, that they derive from a distinct concept of man, of nature, from the same needs and the same inclinations, that they were addressed to the same reigning ideal person and that, finally, they depended upon one another, so that a change in one would bring about a corresponding change in all of them.

A final step needs yet to be made. Until now we have been concerned with the dependencies existing among simultaneous states of affairs; we must next proceed to the conditions involved in successive states. A given epoch is conditioned by preceding ones and it, in turn, imposes conditions upon its successor. One constant in this multitude of factors is the character and spirit of the race. "At a given moment, during a certain period, they produce a creation, and their nature joined to that of their creation, is the *condition* of the creation that follows. . . . The English revolution was produced by the English character and the despotism bequeathed to the Stuarts by the Tudors. The French monarchy of Louis XIV is the result of the French character and the aristocratic anarchy bequeathed to the Bourbons by the civil wars."[35]

Contained in this illustration is already the famous trilogy of race, milieu, and moment which Taine will expose at length in his Introduction to the *History of English Literature* and which he will enlarge upon in *The Origins of Contemporary France*. It must not be forgotten, though, that his explanation of the applied method is a working scheme which will not be exposed in his articles and books where the finished product is presented.[36]

This has led to some confusion. Taine, it is claimed, proposes a method of induction and yet he constantly uses a deductive approach.[37] It is true that M. Pierre and M. Paul demonstrate an inductive method; it is equally true that in his chapter on Stuart Mill, Taine heaps praise on the English philosopher's inductive procedure. But he had taken pains to distinguish the proper use of each method. "The first [induction] is efficacious in physics, chemistry, zoology, and botany, in the earlier stages of every science, and also whenever phenomena are but slightly complicated, within our reach, capable of being modified by means at our disposal. The second [deduction] is efficacious in astronomy, in the higher branches of physics, in physiology, history, in the higher grades of every science, whenever phenomena are very complicated, as in animal and social life, or lie beyond our reach, as the motions of the heavenly bodies and the changes of the atmosphere. When the proper method is not employed, science is at a standstill: when it is employed, science progresses."[38]

The proper method for Taine the philosophical historian would thus be the deductive one, but he obviously uses an inductive-deductive approach. "If he is dealing with a writer or an artist, he *induces* what he must have been like from race, milieu and moment, then, once he has seized the master faculty of his individuality, he *deduces* from it all his acts and works."[39] Taine's inductions are contained in his working notes. The reader is presented with the conclusions drawn from these notes and the deductions derived from these conclusions. This is why he informs us at the outset that Livy was an oratorical historian, Stendhal, a superior mind or that the seventeenth century in France is dominated by an aristocracy of courtiers who conversed in drawing rooms and by an interest in those general ideas for the average man that can be discussed in drawing rooms. If the reader does not agree with the stated cause, he can either verify the deductions derived from it or else do the same reading Taine had done in order to see whether he will arrive at a different cause.

Here we have almost reached the state which Leibnitz envisaged in the distant future: "It is manifest that if we could find characters or signs appropriate to the expression of all thoughts as definitely and as exactly as numbers are expressed by arithmetic or lines by geometrical analysis, we could in all subjects, in so far as they are amenable to reasoning, accomplish what is done in Arithmetic and Geometry. All inquiries which depend on reasoning would be performed by the transposition of characters and by a kind of calculus which would directly assist the discovery of elegant results. We should not have to puzzle our heads as much as we have to-day, and yet we should be sure of accomplishing everything the given facts allowed. Moreover, we should be able to convince the world of what we had discovered or inferred, since it would be easy to verify the calculation either by doing it again or by trying tests similar to that of casting out nines in arithmetic. And if someone doubted my results, I should say to him 'Let us calculate, Sir,' and so by taking pen and ink we should soon settle the question."[40]

VI *At the Threshold of Metaphysics*

Underneath Taine's method are certain beliefs and assumptions which, although not amounting to a system of philosophy, constitute a definite philosophical attitude, and even an outline of metaphysics. Rejecting Kant's limitations imposed on the human mind's capacity of knowing reality,[41] Taine espouses both Spinoza's pantheism and Hegel's rational world view. The joining of these two philosophies (which do indeed have much in common) found its strongest and most lyrical expression in one of Taine's letters written during his first year of teaching:

> Nature is God, the real God, and why? Because it is perfectly beautiful, eternally living, absolutely one and necessary. . . . One part of the world claims another, as one organ of the body makes all others necessary; and the world is one, like the human body. Each part of the world is imperfect, because its complements and the rest of its being is in others, and thus the All is perfect. Those who deny that such a God can be worshipped are ignorant of the enchantments of science. . . . Which is better, when gazing at a landscape, to think of a great gardener's skill, or gaze upon a living Being, resting and developing, and stirring all the sympathies within our hearts?[42]

Much as he respected Aristotle, Spinoza, Hegel and Stuart Mill, Taine was not an uncritical admirer. He applauded Stuart Mill for his painstaking method of induction that never lost sight of facts, but he found that the practical approach of the English philosopher did not go far enough. He was overwhelmed by his reading of Hegel, but he feared that the German philosopher's speculations would leave him with his feet in the air. "We have extended the English ideas in the eighteenth century; and now we can, in the nineteenth, add precision to German ideas. Our business is to restrain, to correct, to complete the two types of mind, one by the other, to combine them together to express their ideas in a style generally understood, and thus to produce from them the universal mind."[43]

Believing that abstraction of factual causes could take over where Stuart Mill's induction leaves off, he envisaged the possibility of going from cause to cause in increasing order of importance until, with the perfection of science, the splendor of the first cause might finally come into view. The purpose of all sciences is to contribute to bringing us closer to that first law of which they are subordinate ones. Each science is concerned with uncovering a specific group of laws and, as it advances, to reduce them to a small number of general propositions from which the rest can be deduced. We shall know nature when we shall have reduced its millions of facts to two or three laws.

One of the accusations often leveled against Taine describes him as a pessimist; this was certainly true of his attitude so far as his own times were concerned, but in the longer view he exuded optimism. "I am anything but a skeptic," he explained to André Chevrillon. "I believe human intelligence has no limits. I think that with sufficient data, such as perfected instruments and continued observation will be able to supply, we can know everything about man and life."[44] In time to come he foresaw all physical sciences merging into mathematics and mechanics; in the human sciences, psychology would play a similar role until finally the sciences could be reduced and induced to the first and supreme law.[45] In anticipating that distant day, Taine reminds us of Faust foreseeing his city built on land regained from the sea, and imploring that perfect moment: "Stay, you are so beautiful!"

Suppose that this work has been done for all peoples and all history, for psychology for all human sciences, for zoology, physics, chemistry, astronomy. At that instant the universe as we see it disappears. All facts have been reduced and replaced by formulas; the world has become simple, science has come into being. All that subsists is five or six general propositions: the definitions of man, of animal, of plant, of chemical body, of physical laws, of astronomical body, that is all. . . .

At such a moment one feels emerging in oneself the notion of Nature. By that hierarchy of necessities, the world forms one single indivisible being of which all beings are members. At the supreme summit of things, at the highest point of the luminous and inaccessible ether, the eternal axiom speaks out and the prolonged echo of this creative formula composes the immensity of the universe through its inexhaustible waves. All forms, all changes, all monuments, all ideas are one of its acts. . . . Indifference, the immobile, the eternal, the all-mighty, the creator, no name exhausts it; and when it uncovers its serene and sublime face, there is no human spirit that does not bow consternated with admiration and horror.[46]

But Taine stopped at the threshold of the Promised Land. At the end of his favorite work, *On Intelligence,* he writes: "Here we have come to the threshold of metaphysics. We do not enter, . . . we only wanted to indicate the probable point, up there well above our heads and our present means, where the key to the vault of the edifice is located."[47]

A belief in a rational, pantheistic universe in which all things are related, being deduced from a supreme and single law; a method based on scientific procedure that amasses all available facts, groups them, finds out the dominant cause of each group and deduces the subordinate factors from this cause; a conviction that the same type of procedure that works in the physical sciences can be applied to human sciences, even though only perfected instruments will permit more accurate measurements in human affairs—these were the assumptions and the method that inspired Taine's work.

VII *Taine's Psychology*

To complete the portrait of a philosophical historian who sought the psychological factors behind people and events, we need to know Taine's views on and achievements in psychology. His contribution in that field was considerable if judged historically, less important when measured against the findings of a Freud, a Jung or an Adler. On the other hand, his efforts to replace metaphysical entities (faculty, capacity, power) by factual explanations carried into psychology the effort he had already undertaken in philosophy. Finally, Taine's conception of man, of normal and abnormal behavior provides us with a key to a better understanding of his criticism in literature, art, and history.

Taine, it will be remembered, had assigned a central place to psychology among the human sciences. His interest in this subject dated from his student days at the Ecole Normale, a number of his major ideas are already contained in *The Nineteenth Century Classical Philosophers,* and if his proposed dissertation on sensations had been accepted in 1852, *On Intelligence* would certainly have been published long before 1870. As it turned out, his doctoral thesis on La Fontaine led him into literary criticism which, along with his courses at the Ecole des Beaux-Arts, left him no time to devote to the work he had contemplated for so long and which was certainly dearest to his heart.

The definition of intelligence Taine proposes makes his work appear more like a modern continuation of John Locke's *Essay Concerning Human Understanding* (1690) than a psychological study: "If I am not mistaken, we mean nowadays by Intelligence, what was formerly called Understanding or Intellect—that is to say, the faculty of knowing; this, at least, is the sense in which I have taken the word. At all events, I here intend to examine our knowledge, that is to say our cognitions, and nothing else."[48] In reality, however, Taine went considerably beyond his predecessors, who had usually based their psychological writings on introspection, by calling to his aid practically all information available at the time. He studied cases of mental illness in medical journals and at the mental hospital in Paris, he utilized knowledge drawn from physiology, neurology, linguistics and ethnography, he observed or consulted children, old people, creative artists;[49] and he carefully noted the effects of hypnotism and somnambulism. The infusion of scientific observation into the field of psychology made of Taine "the leader of the empirical school and the exponent of concrete practical methods of study."[50] Yet, to be complete, *On Intelligence* would have required additional studies dealing with the author's theory of passion and of will.[51]

In psychology Taine applies his philosophical principles that give to *On Intelligence* a unity which, by that very fact, remains based on philosophical rather than experimental foundations. At the core of his work lies the Spinozist assumption he had already expressed in his explanation of cause,[52] namely that the order and connection of things is the same as the order and connection of ideas. In this spirit Taine attempts to supply a scientific answer to the age-old question whether what we perceive corresponds to an exterior reality, a matter that had been severely placed in doubt most recently by Kant.[53] The other important assumption Taine makes is that psychological and physiological phenomena, although different in nature, parallel each other.

After showing that images, signs and general ideas derive all from sensation, Taine deals with a series of problems. What happens when we perceive an object? What is the relationship between interior or psychic and exterior or physiological experience? Does our perception correspond to exterior reality? Perception takes place through two channels: one, sensation, comes from within and takes place without any intermediaries; the other, a molecular movement of the nervous centers, comes from without and through several intermediaries. One may interpret this situation in two ways. Either these two means of perception are perpetually divergent and remain mutually irreducible; or they are basically one and the same event condemned to appear always and irremediably double. If we choose the first hypothesis, we must accept two different worlds, one interior, the other exterior, and seek aid for explanations beyond nature in the supernatural. Leibnitz, realizing this dilemma, had proposed a solution based on preestablished harmony by which God arranges the exact concordance between these two independent channels of perception. Choosing the second hypothesis, which is equally plausible, has the advantage of dealing with a simpler and more convenient relationship, since no imaginary or unknown property is needed to explain it.

This attitude leads to a tendency that views psychological events as problems of molecular movements related to mechanics and hence seeks explanations and solutions in terms of physiology. It is interesting in this respect to compare how Taine and Freud would explain a particular case. Thus Taine attributes loss of memory about a specific period or place in the life of a patient to "an injury, a rush of blood, a deterioration of the blood, any change of the cerebral substance, [which] may hinder or promote the arising of certain groups of images."[54] No doubt, Freud would look elsewhere for an explanation, possibly to an event that happened during that time or at that place which may have created a feeling of guilt in the patient who wishes to repress it.

It would be incorrect to conclude from the foregoing that Taine was unaware of complicated psychological processes. He studied cases of split personality; he knew that, below the surface of psychic experience, there lurks the undefined area of the unconscious or the subconscious; he realized the complexities contained in the concept of the Ego. Here again explanations are suggested in terms of motion, energy and physics. Thus the subconscious is defined as the mental phenomenon which is analogous to the physiological one of audibility. Just as there are limits in terms of decibels to the relative loudness of sounds that the human ear can detect, so there are limits, less accurately measurable, to what the human consciousness can be aware of. "The elementary sensations directly making up our ordinary sensations are themselves compounded of sensations of less intensity and duration, and so on. Thus, there is going on within us a subterranean process of infinite extent, its products alone are known to us and are only known to us in unrefined bulk. As to elements and elements of elements, consciousness does not attain them, reasoning concludes that they exist; they are to sensations what secondary molecules and primitive atoms are to bodies; we have but an abstract conception of them, and what represents them to us is not an image, but a notation."[55]

Having opted for the correspondence of interior and exterior events, Taine might have rested peacefully in the secure feeling that we automatically experience true reality; yet he arrives at quite contrary conclusions. He was painfully aware of the many traps that have to be sidestepped before perception has any chance of mirroring exterior reality. In fact, he substantially agrees with Kant on the deceptive tendencies of our sensations, since they frequently do not correspond to an exterior object (in dreams, under hypnosis, etc.) or else we may misinterpret them (looking into a mirror, for example). Taine goes far beyond these simple errors of the senses by stating that what we perceive is indeed a hallucination. Even if a sensation arises in consequence of its usual antecedent, i.e. after the excitation of the nerve and through the effect of an external object, this sensation, being internal, engenders in us a phantom which we take to be an external object. Thus the hallucination, which seems a monstrosity, is the very fabric of our mental life.[56]

Up to this point Taine arrives by different ways at the same general result as Kant, but he does not stop there. Nature has provided us with antagonist reductives so that, in the normal state of wakening, we can rectify the initial hallucination. They operate by opposing or negating the hallucination through a contradictory representation or sensation. This rectification process takes many forms. The simplest of these are the awakening after a dream, a partial negation through our intelligence of a contradictory proposition (e.g., a figure having three sides and four at the same time) or one sense rectifying the illusion of the other (touching a stick in the water proves that it is not bent). Hence exterior perception is a *true hallucination*. "To form complete hallucinations and repressed hallucinations, but in such a way that, when awake and in the normal state, these phantoms usually correspond to the real things and events, and thus constitute cognition, that is the problem."[57]

But what happens when the rectifying apparatus does not function properly? Then the result is madness of one sort or another, and, since the natural state of hallucination which our sensations induce in us is frequently rectified only by another contradictory hallucination, whose nature is nonetheless the same as that of the initial one, the desirable state constituted by health and sanity turns out to be not only far from normal but extremely precarious:

Our idea of our person is a group of co-ordinated elements whose mutual associations, ceaselessly attacked and ceaselessly victorious, are maintained during our waking hours and reason, as the composition of an organ is maintained during health and life. But madness is always hovering near the mind, as illness is always hovering near the body; for the normal combination is a victory only; it results from and is renewed by the continual defeat of the contrary forces. Now, these last are always present; an accident may give them the preponderance; there is but little required to enable them to assume it; a slight alteration in the proportion of the elementary affinities and in the direction of the constructing process would bring on a degeneracy. Morally or physically, the form we term regular may indeed be the most frequent, but it is through an infinite number of possible deformations that it is produced.

We may compare the silent elaboration of which consciousness is the ordinary result to the progress of the slave, who, after the games of the circus, crossed the length of the arena, among the wearied lions and glutted tigers, bearing in his hand an egg; if he arrived safely, he received his freedom. So passes the mind through the confusion of monstrous deliria and yelling madness, almost always with impunity, to settle itself in accurate consciousness and exact recollection.[58]

The conception of basic human nature which results from this manner of presenting mental processes is anything but reassuring. Time and again, in a cacophonic crescendo, Taine paints a picture of man that leaves him tottering precariously at the brink of threatening insanity. Barely covered by a veneer which required thousands of years of civilizing efforts, the ape lurking constantly beneath and always menacing to burst through his weak bars will supply French Naturalist writers with characters to be dissected in experimental novels.

Man is an animal by nature and by structure, and neither nature nor structure ever loses a single fold. He has the canine teeth like the dog and the fox, he once fastened them in the flesh of his own kind; his descendants cut each other's throat with stone hatchets for a morsel of raw fish. Even now he is not changed; he is only softened. War rages as of old, only it is confined and partial; each one still fights for his morsel of raw fish, only it is under the eye of the policeman and not with stone hatchets.[59]

The foundation of the natural man are irresistible *impulses,* anger, appetites, greed; all blind. He sees a woman, thinks her beautiful; suddenly his throat tightens, heat runs down his back; he rushes towards her; someone tries to restrain him, he kills this man, gluts his passion, then thinks no more of it, save when at times a vague picture of a moving lake of blood crosses his brain and makes him gloomy.[60]

What we call reason in man is not an innate endowment, primitive and enduring, but a tardy acquisition and a fragile composition. The slightest physiological knowledge suffices to show that it is a state of unstable equilibrium, dependent on the no less great instability of the brain, nerves, circulation and digestion.[61]

Studying the behavior of peasants and workers who had been turned into unprofessional soldiers during the French Revolution merely reinforced this basic attitude on man in Taine, for he sees "all of a sudden spring forth the barbarian, and, still worse, the primitive animal, the grinning, sanguinary, wanton baboon, who chuckles while he slays, and gambols over the ruin he has accomplished."[62]

Through an examination of Taine's psychology and his conception of man derived from it we have learned some important matters about the author himself, for we can predict some likely consequences of his attitudes:

(1) We know now what he is going to consider a valid and truthful depiction of human nature, and his great admiration of Shakespeare will not come as a surprise to us.

(2) Taine is bound to be opposed to the view of man as a rational being contained in French Classical literature of the seventeenth century.

(3) Taine's lack of confidence in human nature will inspire in him a political conservatism that will insist on strong police protection. What is unexpected is that, viewing men very much in the manner of Hobbes who compared them to wolves, he did not arrive at the same conclusions as the English philosopher, namely, the need for a despotic ruler, but that he rather advocated a decentralized government. This, however, does not make Taine a greater optimist than Hobbes, who at least had confidence in one exceptional man, whereas Taine saw the best solution in a haphazard system of checks and balances among unbalanced brains.

Before leaving Taine's psychology, a word of caution or at least an admonition to observe historical humility may be in order. It is quite normal to consider Taine's psychological views outmoded today and to feel justly proud of the undeniable progress that has been made in that field since 1870. Yet, in the lottery of time, when Taine's particular physiological explanations of mental processes will long have been consigned to the mothballs of history, his basic principles may yet be vindicated. His misfortune lies in the fact that physiology and neurology have not made the jump forward he had hopefully anticipated. Not that the actual progress accomplished in these sciences is not highly admirable, but the discoveries required to prove Taine definitely right or wrong in his theories of physiological psychology would be of the magnitude that only rare break-throughs can provide. If and when such startling discoveries occur, present-day psychology may in turn be placed on dusty bookshelves as curiosities that filled an intolerable void during an interim period by substituting highly ingenious dramatic characters for what eventually may be explained in terms of glandular secretions, chemical imbalance or genetic irregularities.

Taine himself set a splendid example of scientific humility: "One learns very quickly that what we call an indisputable truth is only a very probable truth; that the idea we have of ourselves and of other things is only a likely hypothesis, well done, useful in guiding our conjectures, the best that have come to us up to now, but perhaps insufficient and temporary, in any case destined to make way for another one when new observed facts, more precise measurements, unexpected connections will enlarge and rectify our conceptions."[63]

Having examined Taine's philosophical views, the method he devised and his psychological attitudes, we are now ready to see how he applied these basic principles to the study of literature, art, and history.

CHAPTER 3

The Literary Critic

Fairness requires that a critic should be judged according to what he proposes to do, and few critics have stated their goals more unequivocally than Taine. Of course, one may reject his method altogether, find it unpleasant, or criticize its philosophical foundations. Perhaps the universe is not rational and unified at all but a jumble of unrelated events; perhaps no relationship between the physical and the human sciences can be established; perhaps the relationship between the artist and society is considerably more complex than Taine suspected; perhaps all our faculties are equally strong with none dominating, perhaps cause and effect are an observed phenomenon without any assured links between them. A convinced Kantian will no doubt find it difficult to accept Taine's premise that "the order and connection of things is the same as the order and connection of ideas."

These are certainly weighty objections which will have to be taken into consideration in evaluating the limitations of Taine's basic assumptions and the method derived from them. But then analogous reservations can be advanced in judging any philosophical stand, since it necessarily excludes those opposed to it. Most serious has been the opposition of literary people who are angered by Taine's manner of using literature as a means of understanding an age or a nation rather than as an end in itself. This deeply ingrained attitude presented a major stumbling block to a sympathetic reading of his best work in his own time, and still at present the same desire to keep literature in a hallowed shrine where critics endowed with personal good taste legislate for the select few or the open-mouthed many continues to oppose all attempts to assign any but a sovereign role to literary works.

I *The Philosophical Critic*

Whatever the merits of this particular attitude may be, it cannot be used to judge Taine. His plea that other methods of literary criticism should at least be given a chance sounds as eloquent to-day as then:

Let us at least tolerate other types of research; let the object that furnished material for depiction furnish material for philosophy; allow analysis to come after art. If it is beautiful to make us see a character, it is perhaps interesting to make us *understand* him. The two types of study are different, since imagination differs from intelligence, and in a reasoning process one has the right to take apart what our eyes have contemplated and our hearts have felt. I may ask myself the question: whence come these qualities, these defects, these passions, these ideas; which of them are effects, which are causes; from what primitive qualities do they spring; whether by pursuing these qualities still further, we may not get to a common source; how much weight and what kind of feelings each of them has contributed to the total passion. Man's emotions and thoughts are linked like parts and movements of the body; and since this chain phenomenon is worthy of note in the corporeal and visible world, it is worthy of note in the invisible and incorporeal world as well. Henceforth all your precepts crumble; the rules that governed depiction have no place in analysis; what would be an error in the former method becomes a duty in the latter. . . . For it the change in purpose has changed all the rest; if its goal is found to be legitimate, one cannot prohibit it from taking the road that leads to that goal.[1]

The "you" in the preceding quotation refers to the famous critic Sainte-Beuve. All his life Taine professed a great admiration for his eminent colleague, but it cannot be considered an uncritical one. At the time of his first Preface to the *Critical and Historical Essays* (1858) Taine had treated him with somewhat doubtful respect, suggesting that Sainte-Beuve was the kind of critic one should savor rather than read. He also never praised the early Sainte-Beuve (*Volupté,* the *Poésies,* and the *Premiers Portraits*). What he appreciated was the psychological historian of the *History of Port-Royal* and the critic of the *Lundis* as the inventor of a method that linked natural history and human history. Sainte-Beuve's greatest contribution to literary criticism can be found in his insistence that the work and the author's biography are inseparable. His natural tendency led him to exaggerate the biographical part, often at the expense of the work itself, but he attempted to discover the deeper causes behind a work of literature by studying the author in his race, through his parents, brothers, sisters, then in his early education; later on, in his literary circle and during his first success; finally, he attempted to uncover the author behind the work and assign him to a particular human group. Yet, when pressed by Taine's systematic criticism to expose his own method, Sainte-Beuve scarcely went beyond a study of the individual. Such terms as "family of minds" to designate a common type of mind throughout history belong far more to the field of literary analogy than to science. Taine, who paid glowing tribute to his colleague upon the latter's death, calling him one of the five or six most useful savants of the human spirit in the nineteenth century,[2] added this remark: "This sort of botanical analysis practiced on human individuals is the only means of bringing together the human and the positive sciences; one only has to apply it to peoples, epochs, and races to make it bear its fruits."[3]

Taine saw in Sainte-Beuve above all the man who had finally introduced psychology into literary criticism. This was the vital first step; the extension of the principle from the individual author to the larger groups and epochs and finally to man in general would be the task of future critics:

The distance between the novel and criticism is no longer great. . . . Formerly, criticism consisted of the impression of a man of taste. . . . In the hands of Sainte-Beuve it has become a study not only of the work but of the author as well; not only the author but the whole man of which the author is only a part. Means have been found to discover his feelings in his work, to sort out his faculties and his tendencies, their order, proportions and degree. His actions and his life, the influence of his times and his country have been joined together, and it has been possible to reconstruct, in the great domain of the past, living people with those prominent and special traits typical of individuals, centuries and races, so that history is being renewed. Thus, if the novel attempts to show us what we are, criticism is attempting to show us what we have been. Both are now a great survey about man, about all the varieties, all the situations, the flourishings, the degenerations of human nature. By their seriousness, their method, their rigorous accuracy, their future and their hopes, both the novel and criticism are drawing close to science.[4]

It should be abundantly clear by now that Taine was not an or-

dinary critic. Actually neither Sainte-Beuve nor Taine concentrated
on the literary work as such: the first saw in it a more or less dis-
guised reflection of the author himself, the second used it as a
document of the past, the study of an epoch or a nation, and of
human nature in general. As he grew older, Taine increasingly
shifted his interest to the extra-literary aspects of criticism: "The
work of art no longer interests me in itself, it is a sign of the deeper causes that have brought it into being. What I am studying in
it is its causes which move me, amaze me, delight me. Consequently, the virtue of arrangement, general harmony, perfect delicacy, supreme measure attract me less than excessive and violent
shocks."[5]

As the object of literary criticism changes, so do the questions
that it seeks to answer. For Taine, these are some of the problems
to which he addressed himself: What is the dominant trait in an
individual author? What have been the persistent traits of a people
or a race? What has been the law of its evolution? Can we infer
general laws about the development of all human beings from these
particular laws? Is it possible to arrive at the definition of a civilization, of a people, of an age? How do literatures, religions, arts,
political societies come into being? How do they grow? How do
they die? Taine as a critic must be judged on his own terms by an
examination of whether he succeeded in offering valid answers to
these questions.

II   *Titles and Style*

Of course, he did not work in an isolated laboratory. He wrote
for magazines; his publisher looked for sales appeal in his books,
hence the title could not sound pedantic. Finally, Taine loved literature profoundly, not just as a document but for its own sake, and
he possessed a brilliant style of writing, quite the contrary of the
dry prose one might expect from a scientific critic.

The first of these factors has led to a great deal of criticism that
can only be called literal-minded. It is easy to find serious omissions in his *History of English Literature* and in his *Philosophy of
Art;* yet, in spite of the titles, neither is intended to be a history,
literary or artistic, in the ordinary sense of the word. A mere perusal of the prefaces leaves no doubt about the intentions of the

author. In fact, most of his works, if the publisher would not have objected, should have carried different titles. The *Essay on Livy* should have been called *An Illustration of Master Faculty through Livy; La Fontaine and His Fables* should have been entitled *On Ideal Beauty, Poetry and the Gallic Spirit as Illustrated by La Fontaine;* the *History of English Literature* might have been renamed *The History of the English Race and Civilization as Seen through English Literature.* A book, as we well know, must be judged neither by its title nor by its ending (nor by its advertising jacket, for that matter), but by its content.

The second factor, Taine's style, presents us with a more complex problem. His success must be partly attributed to his brilliant style, full of striking images and succinct phrases that impress themselves on the mind of the reader. Yet it cannot be denied that this kind of style is more suitable for an impressionistic than for a scientific critic. Trying to be analytical and yet write vividly in the manner of fiction writers created a state of extreme tension in him: "I think I have found the root of my ill. Indeed, my fundamental idea has been that one must reproduce the emotion, the particular passion of the man described, but moreover to expose one by one the degrees of logical generation; in short, to depict him in the manner of artists and at the same time to construct him in the manner of reasoners. The idea is true; besides, when one succeeds in applying it, the effects are powerful. I owe my success to this, but it leaves one's brains disjointed and no one has the right to destroy himself."[6]

Sometimes the artist in Taine wins out over the analytical scientist, but this is not sufficient reason to praise him for being an outstanding critic *in spite of* his method.[7] Surely, no more backhanded compliment could be paid to the author of the *History of English Literature.* He was either a philosophical critic who succeeded in expressing himself artistically or else he amounts to no more than just another brilliant essayist such as Emile Faguet, Jules Lemaître, and the unending series of lesser-renowned producers of flowing prose who filled the literary feuilletons of French newspapers during the nineteenth century.

To evaluate Taine's literary criticism we shall consider three types of study he suggested in his Preface to the *Essays*: that of an individual (Livy, Balzac, Stendhal) will concentrate on the master faculty theory; that of an age (the seventeenth century in France) will deal with the spirit of an age and its ideal man; finally, that of a nation's history will bring into play Taine's oft-quoted tripartite theory of race, milieu and moment.

III   *Master Faculty Defined*

It is not easy to define the exact meaning Taine gave to master faculty.[8] It may be applied both to an individual and to an entire civilization.[9] In either case, however, it represents an effort to find a primal cause or "characteristic and dominant trait from which the whole can be geometrically deduced; in a word, to get at the right formula."[10] This formula, a brief, striking and strong phrase, has necessarily the advantages and disadvantages of that sort of summary: it helps the reader to concentrate on the most important aspect of the author and remember it, but at the same time it will always be incomplete; it may even give the impression of being superficial. We must not forget that the formula is the abbreviated result of successive simplifications; hence its meaning can become clear only in the consequences the critic derives from it.

Taine's *Essay on Livy* (1856) which won a prize reluctantly granted by the French Academy, is, most of all, a thesis designed to prove the author's theory of the master faculty. The formula he uses to summarize Livy's dominant trait is "an orator turned historian." No one has expressed the objections commonly raised to this procedure better than Taine himself:

An orator turned historian: you confine all of Livy to these few words; I am afraid you will suffocate him that way. All Romans are orators and each of them can be distinguished from all the others. This one is a patrician, a patriot, a religious and decent man; he is more sober than Cicero, more regular than Sallust, simpler than Tacitus. He has certain qualities, certain shortcomings, feelings appropriate only to the times he lived in, to the circumstances that formed him, to the type of mind that was his. One stroke may suffice to draw a geometrical figure, but it takes a thousand strokes, criss-crossing each other infinitely, to form a human figure. You thought you were drawing a face; all you have traced is a circle or a square.[11]

After replying that this objection is valid for an impressionistic critic but not for one who tries to be philosophical, Taine proceeds to justify his use of that short formula:

These words (an orator turned historian) contain more aspects than first impression suggests; most of those you thought were omitted are actually included in them: the religious patrician, the decent man and the Roman contributed to forming the orator in him; the events of his times, the fall of the Republic and the establishment of the Empire, placed him into libraries instead of sweeping him to the rostrum and turned him into a historian rather than a statesman. You see that the preceding and following states are attached to the formula. As for the remaining matters, they are indicated by a cursory word; they do not require more space, for they are accidents, and not causes; and since the causes have been seized and followed up, I have all I want.[12]

While the *Essay on Livy* served primarily as a demonstration of Taine's master-faculty theory, his articles on Balzac and Stendhal, pioneer works on both novelists, permit us to examine the theory in practice when applied to a more complex, and hence less ideal, subject matter. Considering that, at the time these articles were published, the authors involved had not yet been thoroughly studied, had in fact received unfavorable treatment from the powerful Sainte-Beuve, one can only admire the insights contained in Taine's articles. Compared with Sainte-Beuve, who grudgingly paid some homage to Balzac only upon the novelist's death and who found Stendhal's novels "detestable," Taine's contribution to a better understanding and appreciation of the two great writers cannot be overestimated.

IV *Master Faculty in Individual Authors: Balzac*

If ever a writer and a critic were made for each other, Balzac and Taine meet this ideal requirement. In pointing to influences on Taine, Balzac tends to be overlooked; yet we find the application of the natural sciences to human affairs prominently stated in Balzac's Preface to the *Human Comedy* (1841), where Cuvier and Geoffroy Saint-Hilaire are repeatedly referred to. What ties the two men even more closely together is Balzac's habit of presenting monomaniacs so completely dominated by their ruling passion that, like Baron Hulot in *Cousin Bette,* they are eventually reduced to a "temperament." Finally, Balzac, as Taine, attempted to introduce unity into the chaos of details by joining his individual novels together through recurring characters, so as to describe an entire epoch.

In Taine's article one searches in vain for indications of a single master faculty from which all of Balzac's other traits could be derived. Rather the critic suggests that two principal aspects provide the key to his works: (1) his temperament, that of a natural scientist whose imagination often carries him away to the point of being obsessed by his fictitious characters, and (2) his life and character: a businessman constantly in debt, a Parisian in manners, wit and inclination, and a personality in which animal vitality abounded.

From the first feature a number of Balzac's strengths and weaknesses derive naturally. He will not depict but dissect, which explains the frequent detailed enumeration of objects in his novels and the accumulation of facts he needs before getting to the subject matter itself. These lengthy introductions irritate readers unaware of the novelist's purposes. He systematically shows how all these factors contribute to a passion or a situation which dominates his characters and which is responsible for all that happens to them. As Balzac is a naturalist,[13] he does not consider man as a specially privileged part of the natural world but a simple force like all others, subject to the same laws. Nor does he see moral virtues in man; he is rather interested in the special type or in a striking abnormality that will disclose new information. Contrary to Corneille, Balzac does not believe that mere will is sufficient to become a hero. "In his view, will has its causes; when a man moves, he has been pushed; some spring in the 'spiritual automaton' has been set in motion and has moved all the rest. For him virtue is a product just as wine and vinegar, excellent indeed, one that you should have an abundance of, but that is manufactured as all other products by means of a series of fixed operations and with a measurable and certain effect. Ordinarily it is but the transformation or the development of a passion or habit: pride, narrow-mindedness, blind obedience, vanity, prejudice, scheming— all lead to it. The vices contribute their share similar to those ill-smelling substances that go into the distillation of the most exquisite perfumes."[14]

Hence it is important to determine which are the forces that act upon man and society. "In the view of the naturalist Balzac, these forces are passion and self-interest. Polite manners embellish them, hypocrisy disguises them, foolishness covers them with nice names, but basically nine out of ten acts are egotistical. And this is hardly surprising. . . . The constant thought of the animal is to nourish and defend itself, and the animal persists in man, with this difference: that, since man's thought is more far-reaching, his needs and dangers are greater. This is why Balzac considers society as a conflict of egoisms where force guided by ruse triumphs, where the torrent of violent passion breaks through the dikes erected to contain it, where accepted morality is limited to the apparent respect of propriety and of the law."[15]

Exposed here, as early as 1858, is already the program French Naturalism will adopt later in the century: the study of man as part of nature, the detached attitude of the author who views his characters the way a medical researcher would deal with an interesting specimen, the determinism of forces that account for man's behavior. Balzac is justly considered to be the father of French Naturalism, but without Taine's intermediary role as a philosophical critic, Balzac's influence on Zola and the other Naturalist writers might not have had the same effect; in fact, without Taine Naturalism would probably have lacked a strong philosophical basis. Not many critics can boast of having written both the first important articles on two literary masters and of having provided a new literary movement with some of its most important ideas.

Do we know Balzac by now? Of course not. So far he merely illustrates the Naturalist writer in literature. We still need to consider an equally important aspect of his work: his life and character. He was a businessman and, Taine hastens to add, a businessman constantly in debt. This explains the importance of money in his novels. He was a Parisian in manners, wit and inclination,[16] stocky, broad-shouldered, full of animal vitality. From such a man we cannot expect a sober, Classical style nor the successful portraits of delicate persons or sentiments. His style is indeed a mixture of strange metaphors often derived from Parisian low wit and he succeeds in describing grotesque, distorted characters (Mlle. Gamard and Big Nanon) or prostitutes (Esther and Josépha) more successfully than angelic creatures (Mme. Claës and Mme. de Mortsauf).

Still, several of Balzac's novels (e.g. *Louis Lambert, Séraphita*) do not fit into these categories, for they display mystical and visionary leanings which do not at all correspond to what one would expect to flow from the pen of a stocky scientist with Parisian manners and an excessive vitality. Taine does not ignore this side of Balzac, either. He had gone through similar experiences himself and, although no trace of Swedenborg's mysticism can be found in his writings, the scientific critic had waxed lyrical and visionary in imagining the time when the first cause would unveil itself.[17] Thus naturalism, materialism and mysticism do not necessarily exclude each other. Historically this unexpected combination can be found in the Manicheans of the third century who maintained that God is a liquid, brilliant and subtle to be sure, which nonetheless impregnates heavy matter.

Balzac was led into mysticism because, contrary to a true scientist, he was not skeptical enough to check the findings at which he arrived by intuition, the instrument used by a novelist. Consequently Taine concludes that the visionary novels of Balzac "complete his work the way a flower completes its plant, that the genius of the artist finds in them his complete expression and his ultimate flowering, that the remainder of his work prepares them, explains them, supposes and justifies them, that a cherry tree must bear cherries, a theoretician theories, and a novelist novels."[18]

Finally, like all great writers, Balzac represents his times. He lived in an age of disillusionment, dominated by the collapse of the Napoleonic dreams and the return of the Bourbon kings under whose reign material preoccupations replaced romantic ideals. The young people of Balzac's time found life ugly and dirty; behind their castles in Spain they saw the debtor's prison and so they discussed life, their century, and their society in the manner of high-living misanthropes. "This is a new sort of amusement which is typical of Paris, Balzac, and the nineteenth century: the philosophy of disgust professed in school or gutter language, amidst broken bottles and official documents, by artists who have become partly financiers, partly sick, and partly scoundrels."[19]

V Master Faculty in Individual Authors: Stendhal

The nearly perfect scientific novelist did not turn out to be closest to the heart of the scientific critic. Balzac did correspond to a great number of his ideals, but the author of the *Human Comedy* lacked refinement, discrimination, and psychological insights, the qualities Taine most admired in Stendhal, his personal favorite.

So numerous are the traits possessed in common by Stendhal and Taine that one often wonders whether the critic, consciously or unconsciously, had imitated the novelist. In their personal life the two men showed a close attachment to the female members of their family; Taine's failing his *agrégation* examination because of his interest in Spinoza strangely resembled Julien Sorel's rejection at the seminary for having spent his time reading Horace and other profane authors. It is no accident either that the young hero of Taine's unfinished novel *Etienne Mayran* exhibits a number of Julien Sorel's traits and was intended to mix in the best Parisian circles once he had reached manhood, just like the principal character of Stendhal's *The Red and the Black*.[20] The affinities between Stendhal and Taine do not end there. One can trace them in Taine's concept of milieu in which climate plays an important role, an idea Stendhal had similarly expressed in his *History of Painting in Italy:* "A human being," he wrote there, "never appears to me other than as the result of what the laws have put into his head and climate into his heart. . . . In the long run climates give rise to temperaments."[21] Like Stendhal, Taine preferred Shakespeare to Racine, in fact, disliked the rational spirit of the seventeenth century in France while being fascinated by the passions openly displayed in the Italian Renaissance. Even in their political views Stendhal and Taine often see eye to eye. Taine's resigned position that a government duly elected by the people is legitimate[22] is mirrored by Stendhal's Lucien Leuwen who "no longer thought about the Republic which is late in coming. And besides, he said to himself, if the French take pleasure in being ruled monarchically and high-handedly, why disturb them?"[23]

Taine likewise shared Stendhal's attitude toward the United States of America, seeing in it hope for greater freedom but fearing at the same time the tyranny of the people. Speaking of President Van Buren's refusal to act upon the justified complaints of the Mormons because he would lose votes in Missouri, Taine comments: "The people are tyrants in the United States; law and the right cause have to give way on occasion before Mr. Everybody; there lies the vice of democracy and, if one were to look only at that side of it, one would be greatly inclined to bless the policeman."[24]

Although Taine's favorite novel was *The Charterhouse of Parma,* which he read and reread forty or fifty times,[25] Balzac had already published an enthusiastic account of that novel in 1840. Taine therefore chose to deal with *The Red and the Black* which had still been largely neglected by the time he wrote his article on Stendhal in 1864; however, his own ideas on the great French novelist had crystallized ten years earlier at which time, in a letter to Guillaume Guizot, dated June 1854, Taine already called Stendhal a superior and very original mind.

In his article this formula of Stendhal's master faculty is reduced to "superior mind," one that, viewing life from high above, depicts only feelings, character traits, the vicissitudes of passion, briefly, the interior life of the soul which interests the psychologist. Obviously the summary term "superior mind" is again an abbreviation that must be expanded for proper understanding: "A man with such a mind is not easily accessible, for one must climb to get to his level. He has no appeal for the common crowd which hates having to make an effort. He does not desire its praise or to be its leader, for it is below him and he would have to stoop down to it. Besides, he is quite content to live alone or in select company; at that level he sees better, farther and more deeply; as he dominates objects, he chooses to observe and depict only those most worthy of interest."[26]

From the master faculty of the "superior mind" thus explained, the most striking facets of Stendhal's art can be derived. Being primarily interested in the interior makeup of his characters, the novelist will eschew exterior circumstances that others would exploit dramatically: duels, executions, escapes will receive scant attention, but the slightest murmur of the heart will be minutely analyzed; in fact, Stendhal transcends the depiction of the individual and presents us with a psychology in action that deals with the human species in general. What will be the style of a superior man? A cool, detached, and delicately ironic one; he even makes affectionate fun of his young, inexperienced heroes. Balzac was wrong to criticize Stendhal's style, for a superior mind strives only to state its ideas clearly and will not let a tempting metaphor interfere with the clarity and directness of what it has to say.

One further consequence of Stendhal's master faculty is that his characters turn out to be superior beings. Not that they are heroes in the Cornelian sense of the word; rather they are remarkable persons who, like their creator, remain aloof and original. Julien Sorel, the principal personage of *The Red and the Black,* is a coherent character because Stendhal has formed him in accordance with a master faculty: an excessive pride coupled with an inventive and ardent imagination. "Consequently we find in him the habit of concentrating constantly upon himself, of questioning, examining himself, of constructing an ideal model for himself to which he compares himself and according to which he judges and conducts himself. Conforming to this model, for better or for worse, is what Julien calls his *duty* which governs his life. With his eyes fixed upon himself, always ready to suspect himself of weakness, to reproach himself for his emotions, he is foolhardy in order not to lack courage, he exposes himself to the greatest dangers for fear of being afraid."[27]

But Julien Sorel, whether one likes him or not, is superior because he creates his own model and his own conduct; it is this originality which places him above the common crowd. Beyond that, Julien Sorel is a great creation because he corresponds to Taine's ideal literary character, one who is neither a general human type, such as he criticized in seventeenth-century French literature, nor a copy of contemporaries, which he disliked in the writers of his own time. On the contrary, Stendhal's personages are real, complex and original, not the sort of heroes we would be likely to meet or imitate but capable of profoundly affecting both our understanding and our curiosity.

VI   *Master Faculty Evaluated*

The advantages of using the master faculty in literary criticism are obvious: it permits an orderly, well-organized manner of analyzing the works of an author by focusing on one salient trait from which all the others can be derived. It also enables the qualified reader to follow the critic's reasoning process by verifying his syntheses and the consequences he develops from them. In the hands of a gifted critic such as Taine this method can lead to excellent results, for his articles on Balzac and Stendhal still hold their own after the numerous studies devoted to these two writers since then. Very few contemporary critics have managed to write more meaningfully about them in so short a space.

Taine's critical approach is far less satisfactory for those who consider the individual literary work as an isolated event largely limited to the author's individual creative genius and who therefore study every aspect of the author's life, the manner in which he transformed his personal experiences or anxieties, the genesis of the work, its structure and private symbolism. This brings us back to the distinction Taine had made between the critic who depicts and the one who wishes to philosophize. Neither method holds a monopoly on criticism; the question should rather be which method is likely to produce the best result in the case of a particular author, and frequently both should be employed.

The deeper problem is just how valid the master faculty is. Its basis, founded on Taine's belief that everything has a cause and that by induction we arrive at elementary causes, is philosophical rather than psychological. Its assumption that human beings tend to be monomaniacs of one sort or another lacks not precedent but proof, since phenomena applicable in botany and zoology do not automatically hold true for the more complicated human species. We may grant Taine that most writers possess distinguishing characteristics which enable the experienced reader to recognize their unsigned works, and that this fact militates in favor of dominant traits. Beyond this, it would be hazardous to set up psychological laws.

Another question concerns the practical advantages of the master faculty. What good does it do us to learn that Stendhal has a superior mind, Saint-Simon a violent sensibility,[28] Michelet passionate inspiration composed of epical and lyrical poetry,[29] George Sand is an idealistic artist,[30] Racine a monarchical poet representing oratorical reasoning,[31] Diderot an erupting volcano,[32] Rousseau a strange, original and superior man who from childhood on carries in him the germs of madness,[33] and Voltaire has the attributes of an apostle and a prophet whose mind can be compared to a precision scale?[34]

The abbreviated summary is, of course, not meant to be used as a convenient catchword that makes further reading unnecessary, but rather as a means of establishing a focal point for critical development. The formula is the most succinct and abbreviated way of expressing the result of increasingly unified inductions. Once obtained, true to Taine's inductive-deductive method, it serves as the starting point from which its deductive consequences are explained. In Taine's overall method the master faculty occupies a very important place because it helps to distinguish writers who have been subject to the same influences of race, milieu and moment; in fact, it partly answers the question asked by superficial critics why two brothers having been formed by identical forces should produce such dissimilar works as the mediocre Thomas Corneille and his brother, the great Pierre Corneille.[35]

The value of the master faculty method lies ultimately in the quality of work that has gone into defining it. If the critic has analyzed his subject correctly and therefore comes up with the correct master faculty, chances are that all else will also be accurate. But what if the critic has committed an error? As in a mathematical equation, the initial mistake will be multiplied through successive steps, so that the procedure looks correct, but the end result turns out to be completely, or at least partly, wrong. This, I believe, happened to Taine in his analysis of seventeenth-century French literature.

VII   *Master Faculty of an Age:*
The French Seventeenth Century

Unfortunately Taine did not write one unified work on the French seventeenth century, but it was an age that preoccupied him greatly from his early readings to his last great historical work. Since his remarks on the Classical age in France are scattered in books *(La Fontaine and His Fables)*, lengthy articles on individual authors (La Bruyère, Mme. de La Fayette, Racine, Saint-Simon, La Rochefoucauld), and short sketches of others, either for the sake of comparison (Boileau, Racine, and Molière in the *History of English Literature*) or to describe the spirit of the times (e.g. Molière in *The Ancien Régime*), it is not surprising to find serious inconsistencies in Taine's depiction and judgment of the age.[36]

Although Taine extends the Classical spirit from Malherbe to Delille, i.e., from the early seventeenth century to the French Revolution, in his literary criticism he deals primarily with the great years of Louis XIV's reign (1661-1685). Judging from his own description of his mind[37] and his method which strives for general laws and, in the moral sciences, for a definition of general human nature, we might well expect Taine to be an admirer of the French Classical spirit. Yet, quite on the contrary, it was without a doubt his greatest *bête noire.* Not that he was unable to understand it or at times describe it brilliantly. Still, in his judgment of the age and of its spirit he usually displayed a negative attitude which even went so far as to make it one of the two causes of the French Revolution. And if, perchance, a paragraph of praise escaped his pen, he soon would catch himself and temper it with blame. When reading Taine on the seventeenth century one rarely has the impression of an impartial scientist who is neither praising nor blaming but only concerned with interesting specimens. On the reasons for this attitude we shall speculate later. Let us first see how he exposes the three factors that determine an age: the reigning model, the spirit of the times, and finally its place between the preceding and the following epochs.[38]

The *honnête homme,* the nobleman of Louis XIV's court who spends his time near the King or in conversations in drawing rooms, is the ideal person to whom all writers and artists address themselves. He has had a good general education, talks well and possesses good sense based on the practical experience that life in an elegant society bestows upon a man:

His talent has reflection for its basis, but it is cultivated by the world. His character has honesty for its basis, but it is in harmony with the world. You may imitate him without transgressing either reason or duty; he is neither a coxcomb nor a roisterer. . . . He will discuss even morality and religion, but in a style so natural, with proofs so clear, with warmth so genuine, that he interests women, and is listened to by men of the world. He knows man, and reasons upon him, but in such brief sentences, such living delineations, such pungent humour, that his philosophy is the best of entertainments. He is faithful to his ruined mistress, his calumniated friend, but gracefully, without fuss. All his actions, even noble ones, have an easy way about them which adorns them; he does nothing without diversion. His great talent is knowledge of the world; he wears it not only in the trivial circumstances of everyday life, but in the most moving scenes, the most embarrassing positions.[39]

Under a strong pressure of this kind the mind necessarily accommodates itself to the exigencies, the proprieties, the tastes, and the degree of attention and of instruction of its public. Hence the classical mould, —formed out of the habit of speaking, writing and thinking for a drawingroom audience.[40]

The Classical spirit, which corresponds and responds to this reigning model, situates itself midway between the patient, minute observations of the English and the lofty speculations of the German philosophers. Its strength lies in explanation and clarification, in placing ideas within the reach of everybody through a step-by-step method, so that each new development follows logically from the preceding one. It extracts from each object not the peculiarities that lend individuality to it but some general aspect that can be easily understood. "Its effort consists in fixing the meaning of general terms, its work in establishing the order of general ideas, its merit in going beyond restricted truths but stopping short of metaphysical truths; its name is oratorical reason and its glory to compose beautiful speeches."[41]

What will be the effect of this spirit on the great institutions of the country? Above all, a lack of originality. None can be found in religion: Fénelon, Bossuet, Bourdaloue, Nicole, La Bruyère, all explained and justified faith in admirable discourses, and reworked psychology, history and politics to fit religious dogma. They do not create, they prove, develop and plead; they are the orators of Christianity. Taine pays scant attention to Jansenism (even though his colleague Sainte-Beuve had devoted a lengthy study to this religious movement) and quietism, both of which caused a considerable stir during the seventeenth century.

In philosophy the same spirit can be observed. Descartes contributed no original idea;[42] his metaphysics and proofs are derived from St. Thomas Aquinas, St. Augustine and St. Anselm. His contribution lies in his method and his style, that is to say, in the art of finding the proper order and the exact expression. But, we may object, what about Descartes' methodical doubt, his opposition to scholastic entities which seems so close to Taine's own views? Highly overrated, we are told. Descartes pretends he has abandoned all his previous beliefs, but this is merely an involuntary, or perhaps even an intentional device to lead the reader on. True, Descartes did conceive the world in terms of movement and extension, but he did so merely because his demand for clarity was incompatible with the scholastic beings of his predecessors. Taine leaves us with the impression that French philosophers are incapable of constructing a system of metaphysics and limited to classifying, organizing and popularizing original ideas conceived elsewhere.

One wonders why Descartes is considered to be the father of modern philosophy.

Turning to letters, Taine finds the same oratorical reason dominating there. Written conversations and the desire to speak perfectly, no passion, no new ideas, no brilliant images, but the continuity of thought, the proper expression and the harmony of sentences—this is how he sums up literature in seventeenth-century France. Hence poetry is practically nonexistent; this is an age of prose, effective not in the novel, which requires inventiveness, but in speeches, sermons, polemics and intimate letters. In this realm the century has no equal.

In the theater, oratorical reason produced inevitable effects. The main concern of the dramatic author is the plan, the structure of the play. He must obey the rule of unity of time, place and action; nothing improbable must mar the action; there must be no violent scenes on stage; and the dramatic verse must conform to the official form of couplets in alexandrine meter. A play like *Hamlet* would be considered an absurdity. The characters are abstract beings rather than real persons. The author is not concerned with his characters' past or the way they came to be what they are now; he picks out a simple passion, say pride, jealousy, marital fidelity, and gives it a soul. As philosophy developed general ideas, so the theater develops general, pure qualities. This is why Classical characters are heroic and attractive. Passion occupies only a secondary function and must be defeated; disorder and madness are not permitted; anything excessive or despicable may not be included, even the villains must be presented with moderation and decency. "If Racine or Corneille had framed a psychology, they would have said with Descartes: Man is an incorporeal soul, served by organs, endowed with reason and will, living in palaces or porticos, made for conversation and society, whose harmonious and ideal action is developed by discourse and replies, in a world constructed by logic beyond the realms of time and space."[43]

The final trait of this theater is eloquence; in fact, the entire play is made up of perfect speeches by characters who are masters in the art of pleasing, convincing, and of maintaining their dignity in all situations. They die with all the proprieties while pronouncing an academic phrase; they plead their passion; they even reason when they are supposed to be delirious. The best thing is to take

French Classical tragedy like opera; in the latter one sings an aria to express sentiments, in the former, tradition demands that one plead one's emotions rationally.

This is fundamentally, with many variations, how Taine depicts the spirit of the seventeenth century. Here he calls its master faculty "oratorical reason"; in his last historical work he will call it "reasoning reason." But with the exception of a few passages which show that he was in no way incapable of penetrating into the splendid sophistication of the century,[44] Taine consistently deprecated what traditionally has been considered the most glorious literary century in France, one that produced Corneille, Molière, Racine, La Fontaine, Pascal, La Rochefoucauld, La Bruyére, Boileau, Mme. de Sévigné and Mme. de La Fayette, to mention only the greatest authors.

VIII   *Racine as Representative of the Age*

What is still more surprising is that the foregoing analysis of the spirit of the seventeenth century served as an introduction to the criticism of Racine's theater. Just as Descartes was denied the ability to produce a metaphysical system in philosophy, so Racine is described as being incapable of feeling or portraying strong emotions. What emerges from Taine's portrait is the gentle, wigged Racine the Romantics had set up as a whipping boy and whose effigy (or wig) had to be burnt to give way to the new theater of Victor Hugo and Alexandre Dumas the Elder. While this attitude is understandable in Victor Hugo, who, after all, was not a critic and who quite properly felt he had to diminish the overwhelming prestige of the Classical theater in order to obtain a fair hearing for his own, the echoing of these views in Taine is far more disturbing.

After reading the critic's recital of Racine's life, one is indeed ready to agree that this man was not likely to produce an intensely emotional theater. Compared to Sophocles or Shakespeare, who lived passionate lives, Racine's seems that of a talented and docile student who enjoyed a smooth career because he had learned the proper manners and wrote what he knew would please his audience. "He never experienced the poignant sensations or the savage fever of original and solitary inventiveness; he is far more a writer than a poet. . . . His correspondence, his entry into society, show a good-humored young man, a good talker, graceful in compliments, possessing none of the peculiarities and violent outbursts which normally are the marks of an artist."[45] And his obedience to Mme. de Maintenon's wishes, his letters to his son, complete the picture of a perfect monarchical poet.

The only trouble with this idyllic presentation of an unruffled, dutiful life is that it makes practically no mention of the years during which Racine wrote his greatest tragedies; we learn only what he was like before *Andromache* and after his retirement from the theater, for all practical purposes, in 1677. Taine does mention one or two slips on Racine's part and the fact that he sowed his wild oats with La Fontaine in Paris. But not a word about the Racine who took away the actress Du Parc from Molière nor about his long affair with another actress, La Champmeslé. His break with his former Jansenist mentors over his plays and his acrimonious letter on this subject are lightly dismissed, and the fact that he retired from the theater in bitterness after having been subjected to chicaneries of various sorts is not even mentioned. Surely, a dramatic author who bows out at the height of his career is not a very common event in the history of the theater. If he did not publicize his love affairs or give vent to his feelings but instead accepted his fate and, after retiring from the theater, devoted himself to his family and to his work as historiographer, that is all to his credit. But what is not committed to private correspondence or to intimate diaries is nonetheless present in a man's heart, and this corrected portrait of Racine, a great deal of which was not unknown to Taine, leads us to conclude that the great dramatist experienced intense emotions, but that he did not choose to display them publicly, an attitude quite in keeping with the exterior dignity his time demanded.[45a]

Once this understatement of passion is understood, it follows that the problem for the modern audience becomes one of inflation of language. And to convert Racine's restrained expressions into the bombast of Romanticism, one would have to amplify his subdued tone by the factor of one hundred, the process of linguistic devaluation paralleling that of financial devaluation since the seventeenth century. That Taine knew this very well is apparent from his judgment of Mme. de La Fayette's style:

This style is as measured as it is noble; instead of exaggerating, it at-

tenuates. Madame de La Fayette never raises her voice. In her uniform
and moderate tone there is no passionate or brusque accent. Throughout her book [*La Princess de Clèves*] a charming serenity shines, her
characters seem to glide through a limpid and luminous air. Love, atrocious jealousy, the supreme anxieties of a body wrecked by the illness
of the soul, the troubled cries of passion, the discordant noise of the
outside world, all is softened and faded out. And the tumult from below rises harmoniously into the pure region we have reached. The
reason is that anything excessive and vulgar is shocking. One does not
shout in a drawing room, and Mme. de La Fayette does not let herself
go like an artist or an actress; she contains herself like a great lady and
a woman of the world. Besides, even a mere hint, especially a mere
hint, is understood by her guests. People who like loud voices have unrefined nerves or dull minds; for her guests a smile, a trembling in the
stress of a word, a slowing down in speech, a fleeting glance suffice.
They guess what is not said and understand what is implied. In their
delicate and prompt grasp of the conversation they perceive, immediately and effortlessly, what is being hidden and what is left unsaid.
They understand or imagine the rapture or the tempest hidden behind
regular and calm sentences. They don't want to see them. They glance
at them and, at the same time, turn their eyes away: they want to keep
their self-control. They know they are being watched, they would
dread being disconcerted by descriptions that are too vehement. Their
refinement does not need them, their dignity is afraid of them, their
good taste keeps its distance from them.[46]

One could not ask for a more delicate insight into the spirit of
the seventeenth century in France. The man who understood Mme.
de La Fayette so well was obviously torn between his literary perceptiveness and his theory on the century. How else are we to explain the startling contradictions within a few pages in the article
on Racine? On page 153, Taine insists that Racine is a writer
rather than a poet; on page 158, we learn that the pure and profound source of his poetry springs from his delicacy and vivacity
of feelings. On page 155, Racine's heart and mind are completely
monarchical; on page 161, we read that "he had the manners of a
courtier but not a courtier's soul," which would imply that Racine's
heart and soul were at odds. The result is a hybrid portrayal of
the great dramatist as both passionate and gentle, a scribbler and
a poet, moderate in everything yet with a soul "that makes great
artists, delicate, excessive, disturbed and unhappy, but from time
to time overcome with gentle sweetness and raptures of which the

rest of humanity has no idea."[47] What has become of his master faculty as a court poet and of the century's master faculty of oratorical reason?

Similar contradictions and omissions can be found in Taine's analysis of Racine's theater. It is true that, since that time, Racine has been the subject of many studies which have discovered ever greater depths in this author,[48] but even by 1858, when Taine wrote his article, the Romantic attacks against Racine had lost their force and a return to neo-Classicism had followed the decline of the Romantic theater. Yet Taine's criticism of Racine could, in great part, easily have been incorporated in Victor Hugo's *Preface to Cromwell* (1827). After assuring us that Racine's characters are abstract beings representing general and simple passions, the critic agrees that they are modeled on contemporaries.[49] While praising Stendhal for not exploiting sensational scenes (duels, executions, violent actions), he finds it difficult to accept the Classical theater's abhorrence of "the exact imitation of death and murder, legs that collapse, and the man on the ground gasping his last breath, the convulsive hiccup caused by poison that is destroying the body, the sobs of a throat being strangled, the feet furiously pounding the floor, eyes that seem to jump out of their sockets and turn white, the agony of sweating and clenched fists."[50]

But most disturbing for today's reader is Taine's treatment of love and passion in Racine's theater. Passion in the seventeenth century, as previously characterized by Taine, may be only a secondary factor that must suffer defeat. In love, the critic claims, "the senses seem not to participate; one does not speak of it, not even to triumph over it, as in Corneille. It is only a sublime and more tender friendship that is satisfied, provided a similar friendship is obtained in return."[51] Even this tender friendship is denied to men; only Racine's women may lay claim to it, and what they love in the man of their choice is his rank.

Are there no madmen, no villains in Racine? Taine smiles at the rational fury of Orestes who does not forget the diplomatic proprieties of an ambassador and who even reasons with the Furies. He has a few kind words for Nero who, being a gentleman, masks his villainy better than Richard III. His preferred female character is Monime in *Mithridates,* for whom he feels an affection mixed with respect. Thus the gentle Racine "is the greatest creator of feminine delicacy and devotion, of aristocratic pride and dexterity. Everywhere one finds refined emotions of wounded bashfulness, little traits of modest pride, hidden avowals, insinuations, . . . veiled coquetry, then touching displays of generosity."[52]

Is he talking about the same Racine we know? One may indeed find fault with the great dramatist, but how can one complain of a lack of passion in his plays where the characters resemble lions in a cage with only two ways out: complete abandonment to the other's passion or death? Did the polite language prevent Taine from realizing that Pyrrhus is using Andromache's son for blackmailing and that he is, in fact, saying to her: "Madame, unless you give yourself to me body and soul, I shall turn your son over to the Greeks who will kill him"? The same holds true of Bajazet whom Roxanne gives the choice between being her lover or being killed. And no amount of reasoning, no appeal to reputation, rank or propriety prevents Pyrrhus from marrying Andromache, Orestes from planning to abduct Hermione, or Hermione from plotting Pyrrhus' assassination. The great women in Racine's theater (Hermione, Roxanne, Agrippina, Phaedra) resemble in almost no way those bashful maidens Taine describes. They are the preys of their passion, and a terrible fate befalls the man who has kindled their desires, for chances are he will not leave the lions' cage alive.

Just as in Racine's life he had slighted the dramatist's great period, so, in analyzing his works, Taine skims over his first success, a work Sainte-Beuve considered very important for the study of an author. In *Andromache* passion turns to blindness or madness and, if Taine finds Orestes too reasonable in his delirium, this opinion would hardly have been shared by the portly actor Montfleury whose death is said to have been caused by the exertion this role demands.

Phaedra, by many critics considered Racine's greatest play, receives equally cavalier treatment. All Taine has to say about this passionate woman is that she dies pronouncing an academic phrase. And yet, what an interesting study in determinism Phaedra might have offered as a woman whose race and heredity is such that, contrary to her good intentions, she succumbs to her powerful drives. In 1858 no one was better qualified than Taine to realize that Racine was not using mythological relationships simply for the sake of creating the celebrated verse which informs us that Phaedra is the daughter of Minos and Pasiphaë.

Taine's article on Racine embodies his concept not only of the seventeenth⁾ century but of the entire French nation, for he calls Racine a national poet, such as Shakespeare and Sophocles, one who mirrors the kind and the degree of French feelings and faculties and who is the best interpreter of the heart for the French. In the light of Taine's attitude that the greater a poet is the more accurately he represents his race and epoch, one might have been justified in expecting a far more appreciative and admiring judgment of the Classical dramatist, but Taine had drawn a distinction in his work on La Fontaine that demotes Racine to a rank below that of the famous fabulist:

The more perfect a poet is the more national he is. The more deeply he penetrates into his art the more he penetrates into the genius of his century and of his race. . . . By this interrelationship of work, country and century, a great artist is a public man. This is what determines his measure and his rank . . . so that he should be considered as the representative and the epitome of a spirit from which he receives his dignity and his nature. If that spirit is merely a fashion and reigns only for a few years, the writer is a Voiture. If that spirit takes a literary form and governs an entire age, the writer is a Racine. If that spirit is the very backbone of the race and reappears in each century, the writer is a La Fontaine. Depending on whether that spirit is temporary, secular, or eternal, the work is temporary, secular, or eternal, and we may express poetic genius, its dignity, formation and origin by saying that it is a summing up.[53]

This praise of La Fontaine represents more than the enthusiasm of a dissertation writer for his subject. In the revised version of *La Fontaine and His Fables* (1861) the fabulist is called the best representative of the true French character: the Gaul. The two qualities of the Gaul, sobriety and quick-wittedness, turn him away from exaltation and poetry and lead him to prose, raillery and narration. What he wants above all is to laugh at the expense of others. "This race is the most Attic of the modern ones, less poetic than the ancient one but as sharp-witted, endowed with an exquisite rather than a great mind, with taste rather than genius; sensuous but without coarseness or fiery passion, not at all moral but sociable and gentle, not meditative but capable of attaining ideas, all ideas, including the loftiest, through banter and gaiety."[54]

Along with La Fontaine, Rabelais, Molière and Voltaire embody this Gallic spirit.

Of course, Gaul was conquered by the Romans and the Latin genius strongly modified the basic Gallic strain of the French race. Even La Fontaine was influenced by Latin culture and his century from which he took his elegant and polite tone, but what matters to Taine is what distinguishes him from the spirit of the seventeenth century: that he was a poet, more than any other Frenchman, that he was carefree, frivolous and amoral, and that his art is popular. This attitude is in part the result of Taine's insistence that the basic character of a race be present in a work at all times, even though modified by other factors. Now, if we compare his description of the spirit of the seventeenth century with that of the Gallic spirit, it is apparent that the Latin culture has almost completely covered the basic Gallic characteristics during that age. We shall have occasion to note, in the *History of English Literature,* that Taine tends to be severe on writers or periods that stray too far from the basic patterns of the race. His preference for the Gallic spirit over the Classical one is no doubt also due to his personal likes and dislikes, yet, in a larger sense, he is consistent in placing the Gallic La Fontaine, who represents the Frenchman throughout the ages, ahead of the Classical Racine who, as representative of only an exceptional period, illustrates a less permanent tendency which will, in turn, enter the total stream of characteristics that are grafted upon the basic nature of the race.

While Taine's admiration for La Fontaine may be justified, his choice of the other two authors on whom he bestows the title of artist is revealing: Pascal and Saint-Simon. The former, his individual greatness as a writer and thinker notwithstanding, represents neither the Gallic spirit nor the major trends of the seventeenth century; the latter was ten years old when the revocation of the Edict of Nantes (1685) signaled the downhill movement of Louis XIV's reign. Since La Fontaine too corresponds only to a minor trend,[55] the conclusion that must be reached is that for Taine the greatest writers of the seventeenth century were not its most perfect representatives but those who were outside of its mainstream. If we add that another favorite of his, Stendhal, wrote in deliberate opposition to most of the trends of his time and country, Taine's theory which equates greatness and representativeness turns out to be seriously jeopardized by his critical practice.

IX   *General Criticism of French Classicism*

Taine's criticisms of the seventeenth century in France are dou-
bly instructive, for they reveal at the same time his concept of an
ideal author. For the Classical period this would be a combination
of La Fontaine and Saint-Simon. Taine's attitude becomes clear
once we recall his definition of poetry as "the art of transforming
general ideas into small perceptible facts and to gather together
the small, perceptible facts to form general ideas, so that the mind
can feel its thoughts and think its sensations."[56]

Of the two demands contained in this definition, the French
Classical writers satisfy at best one (general ideas), and imper-
fectly at that, since Taine depicts them as exposing general ideas
which are not the fruit of small, perceptible facts. In short, Taine
accuses French Classicism of neglecting observation, experience
and experiments. "The classic simply cannot see. Always measured
and rational, his first care is to proportion and arrange. He has his
rules in his pocket and brings them out for everything. He does
not rise to the source of the beautiful at once, like genuine artists,
by force and lucidity of natural inspiration; he lingers in the middle
regions, amid precepts, subject to taste and common sense."[57]
Saint-Simon succeeds in describing an individual with all his peculiarities, whereas "everybody knows that the defect of our Classical poets is to put on the stage not men but general ideas; their
characters are abstract passions that walk and dissertate."[58]

The model is La Fontaine whose manner illustrates Taine's
definition of poetry. The critic's enthusiasm breaks through his
analysis as he describes the perfect poet:

He was of his time, he depicted the men who surrounded him such as
they were. All I needed to do was to assemble traits here and there,
and a whole society was created. La Fontaine took us to Versailles; we
caught a glimpse of Louis XIV in his royal coat, the lords bowing low
in the antechamber, courtiers managing to make off with a retirement
income or a reversion, the bourgeois behind their counters or in their
city halls, the priest rattling off his mass, the peasant at work, tired
and stiff in his work coat full of holes. . . . That is the first virtue of
poetry: give it an idea, it turns the idea into a man; bring it a frame,
it supplies the picture.[59]

It is true that the Classics' lack of interest in nature and their restricted vocabulary had the effect of practically eliminating lyrical poetry as a genre for more than a century, and this is a most deplorable shortcoming. But Taine makes little of this; instead he returns to claiming that Racine and his contemporaries created their characters out of whole cloth by adding arms and legs to abstract passions. Considering that the French Classical authors frequented the court, an ideal place to observe behavior, it would be difficult to deny them a knowledge of the human heart.[60] It is thus rather to the way they express this experience that Taine objects. Yet the very Classical rules of theater obliged them to eschew the exposition of how their characters acquired their psychological makeup, but rather to deduce from a given master faculty (jealousy, hypocrisy, avarice, lust for power) how they will act in a given set of circumstances. No one was better qualified than Taine to appreciate this very method he employed himself in his criticism of individual authors.

Upon examining the reasons for this apparent contradiction in Taine, we find, lurking behind the literary critic, the psychologist who is interested in case studies. What he praises in Saint-Simon's style is not elegance of art but naturalness: "This bizarre style, excessive, incoherent, overcharged, is nature's own expression; none is more useful for the study of the history of the soul; it is the literal and spontaneous notation of feelings."[61] Once more La Fontaine illustrates the kind of writing Taine prefers; in fact, there is a strong indication that he would have applauded the "stream-of-consciousness" technique of James Joyce: "[La Fontaine] hears shaded stresses, a voice that fades in and out; he sees bits of landscapes, gestures, comic or touching figures, and all this as if in a dream. During that time his hand has written unfinished lines concluded with similar syllables, and it turns out that these lines are the same as his dream; his sentences have but noted down emotions. That is why we see emotions through his sentences."[62]

X *Conditions of the Age and Conclusion*

So far the seventeenth century in France has been considered as an age that illustrates the interdependence of its various functions and organisms. It remains now for us to study the conditions of

the period, that is to say, those it inherited from the past and the
ones it passed on to the following century. Taine deals far more
with the latter phenomenon than with the former. One aspect, the
character and spirit of the French race, has already been touched
upon. The other factor, the political and social one (the monarchy
of Louis XIV), Taine explained as having been caused by the
combination of the French character and the anarchy of the nobles
which was responsible for lengthy civil wars and made the French
look with eager anticipation to the majority of Louis XIV.

As the historian of the French Revolution Taine devotes necessarily far more attention to the effect the Classical spirit exerted
on the eighteenth century. Taine's thesis states that the seventeenth-
century authors (Boileau, Corneille and Racine, among others)
are the direct forerunners of Saint-Just and Robespierre, and that
oratorical reasoning produced Rousseau's *Social Contract* and the
Declaration of the Rights of Man. What was needed to bring about
these transformations of ideas was a breaking down of religious
and monarchical dogma through its own excesses, and the new
scientific world view of Newton as popularized by Voltaire. We
shall have occasion to return to this matter in the chapter on
Taine's historical work.

What are we to conclude about Taine's estimate of the seventeenth century in France? First of all, that, as usual, his presentation is brilliant in illustrating the interdependence of seventeenth-
century thought and institutions and that he offers a number of
profound insights into the age. Taine's failing stems not from his
definitions but from a personal attitude which prevented him from
living up to the ideal of the scientific critic: a detached analysis
which accepts facts for what they are and does not attempt to put
a stamp of approval or disapproval on them but rather to sift out
what is characteristic and helpful for our understanding of them.
By denying French seventeenth-century philosophers any metaphysical competence Taine denigrated the important role Descartes played in modern philosophy; by denying the ability to experience or portray passion to seventeenth-century authors, Taine
clung to a judgment of Racine that accepted the worst prejudices
of the Romantics, even to the point of ignoring evidence to the
contrary.

The real trouble with Taine's analysis lies not in the term "oratorical reasoning" but with his interpretation of it. What the critic does not bring out sufficiently (although he occasionally touches on it) is the long and patient refining process that personal experience and observation had to undergo before the Classical authors considered them worthy of public presentation. For the psychologist an unrefined emission of feelings would no doubt be more valuable, and one can sympathize with Taine's frustration of being unable to penerate into the personal depths of the French Classicists. But each age has its own way of expressing itself and the philosophical and historical critic has no choice but to accept it.

Thus, because of a partial and partly faulty interpretation of master faculty, Taine arrived at an equally defective description of the seventeenth century in France; and this defect pervades most of his writings on the subject. It should be remembered, however, that this partial failure does not condemn the method itself but only its particular application.

CHAPTER 4

Race, Milieu, Moment

The History of English Literature was Hippolyte Taine's most ambitious literary undertaking. Having studied the individual author by means of his master faculty, and a century through the spirit and the reigning model of the time, he was now ready to tackle the literary history of an entire nation. Of all his theoretical writings the Introduction to the *History of English Literature* represents the most complete and best-known expression of his critical ideas. Any student of literature automatically associates the famous trilogy of race, milieu and moment with the name of Taine. Yet these terms have given rise to so much misunderstanding that a special effort must be made to render them as clear as possible.

Basically, Taine is dealing with relatively simple concepts. In writing the history of English literature, he attempts to define the English national character or the English spirit, as he calls it.[1] In order to follow that nation through its various stages of development, he had to determine what its permanent features are, which exterior factors had exerted their influences on them, and what state these combined forces had reached at any given time. For these are the three primordial forces responsible for that elementary moral state which affects any writer. More than that, the writer expresses this moral state, and the better he does so the greater he is. The result is an unusual literary history based on generalities that are particularized through great men.[2] Once this is properly understood, the accusation of incompleteness either because of omission of individual writers or of minor tendencies becomes inapplicable.

I Race

By race, Taine means an internal character and temperament so strong that it will indicate parentage even if exterior circumstances interfere and bring about radical changes as in the case of the Aryan race. Taine offers two definitions of race, one abstract, the other historical:

General characters arrange themselves in stages, one above the other, and in proportion as their presence becomes more universal, their contents decrease. At the lowest point is the momentary fact, absolutely singular and distinct, which forms the element of the rest; every moment, action, state, or fact, is thus a prodigiously complex datum, differing from every other, and having its special shade of character. This shade of character subtracted, there remains a cluster of characters common to a whole series of facts, and whose persistence forms the individual. If from this cluster we omit all personal characteristics, the remainder forms the race, that is to say a character present in the individual and in many others. An extract from this remainder is the genus, that is to say a character present in many species; and so on.[3]

If you consider in turn the leading races from their first appearance up to the present time you will always find in them a class of instincts and of aptitudes over which revolutions, decadences, civilization have passed without having affected them. These aptitudes and these instincts are in the blood and are transmitted with it; in order to change them a change of blood is necessary, that is to say an invasion, a permanent conquest, and consequently, comminglings of race, or, at least, a change of the physical *milieu,* that is to say an emigration and the slow effect of a new climate, in short a transformation of temperament and of the physical structure. When, in the same country, the blood remains nearly unmixed, the same character of spirit and of mind which shows itself in the former grandfathers is again found in the latest grandchildren.[4]

Obviously Taine's concept of race is that of the nineteenth century; as early as 1850 he defined it as the character transmitted by the blood, hence hereditary. Viewed from the twentieth century (which is far from having solved all the problems concerning race, heredity and environment), Taine's idea of race strikes us as literary rather than scientific. Besides genetic heredity, he believes that characteristics, acquired due to strong external pressures, such as climate, are passed on to future generations, a view that still enjoyed a great deal of prestige in Russia in the 1960's, "so that at any moment we may consider the character of a people as an abridgment of all its preceding actions and sensations. . . . This is no simple spring, but a kind of lake, a deep reservoir, wherein

other springs have, for a multitude of centuries, discharged their
several streams."[5]

From the foregoing it becomes apparent that for Taine race,
as cause, is a concept that has successive layers of depth. It may
refer to a nation, a subdivision of race (Germanic, Latin), a basic
race (Aryan, Semitic) or the human species as a whole. In the
History of English Literature the author uses the procedure of illustration by contrast, comparing of course the English and the
French and, on a deeper level, the Germanic and Latin races; in
fact, we shall see that this great work contains a secondary thesis
which shows a decided preference for a certain type of Germanic
mind over the Latin character and aptitudes.

Taine applies the term "race" interchangeably with "national
character" to the English, the French or the Germans. We have
already noted the major characteristics he assigns to the French.[6]
Taine's various summaries of the English race are not free of contradictions. Now they are "of a cold temperament, slow to love,
prone to brutal drunkenness," now they display "cold passions";
at one time they are meditative dreamers, at another time, practical; immoral during the Renaissance, they become highly moral
under Puritanism. Certainly, some of these inconsistencies are due
to a lack of overall control by the author, but in a number of cases
they can be explained as being caused by changing conditions, for
it must be remembered that two more factors, beside race, produce
their effects on human beings. The principal characteristics Taine
attributes to the English throughout their history consist of: *(1)* a
strong imagination: fantasy, a passionate sensibility, a lyrical exaltation, a feeling of the sublime; *(2)* concentrated passion: profound
desires, instinct of revolt; *(3)* a positive and practical attitude; *(4)*
a serious, meditative and sad character that tends to turn inward;
(5) the ability to reproduce impressions accurately and minutely;
(6) a moral outlook.

II *Milieu*

To race, the internal mainspring, must be added milieu, the external pressure. Milieu consists of the physical or socio-political
circumstances which counteract or complete the basic character of
the race. Of these, climate is the most important, for, in large part,

it is responsible for such profound differences as exist between the Germanic, on the one hand, and the Greek and Latin races, on the other, all of which were once united in the Aryan race. The cold and humid country and the violent ocean have inclined the Germanic races to melancholic or violent sensations, to drunkenness and heavy eating, to an active life; the Latins, living in beautiful lands bordered by a calm ocean, have adopted a social life and developed the art of conversation; they possess the talent of enjoying life and have attained a high level in science, art and letters. So powerful is the effect of climate that, in its adaptation to it, the race undergoes permanent changes.

Political circumstances leave their traces too, as demonstrated by the two Italian civilizations: the first engaged in action, conquest, government and legislation due to an armed aristocracy forced into systematic war by its very conquests; the second, unable to achieve unity because of its municipal form, the papal presence and foreign intervention, turned toward the cult of voluptuousness and beauty. Finally, social and religious conditions have left their marks. Both Christianity and Buddhism are a reaction to conquests, intolerable oppression, the crushing of the individual, and complete despair which resulted in the development of metaphysics and dreams, renunciation, charity, gentleness, a sense of human fraternity. In India it led to the idea of universal nirvana, in Europe to that of God the father.

Milieu, which Taine defines elsewhere as "the general state of mind,"[7] plays an important role in determining what kind of artistic works are produced during a given period. When that state is melancholic, an artist who might wish to express joy would find himself confronted by so many obstacles that his efforts are likely to be vain or of little influence.

III   *Moment*

The third principal cause Taine calls moment. The term leads to misunderstandings and, in English, equivalents such as "time," "epoch" and "momentum" have been suggested. The last of these corresponds most closely to Taine's view, since he describes this factor also as acquired speed. A similar attitude, which held that an epoch derives from the preceding one and shapes, in turn, the one that follows, had already been expressed in his treatment of centuries. Thus the moment which must be taken into account in the history of a nation or race consists not just of its situation at that particular time but of the accumulation of all its past experiences. French tragedy in the eighteenth century shares a general conception of this genre with the seventeenth, but it is not the same because Corneille was the precursor and Voltaire the successor, because the former had not a distinct model and the latter did, because some aspects of art have been perfected, in short, the first work has determined the second.[8]

The interplay of these three primordial factors is seen by Taine as a mechanical problem, not measurable in exact quantities as in the physical sciences yet one that is made up of forces, magnitudes and directions, and in which the final result corresponds to the factors that produced it. These component parts may work harmoniously or counteract each other to produce either brilliant triumphs or impotent epochs. As an example of triumphs Taine cites seventeenth-century France (somewhat of a surprise in view of his general attitude toward that period), when the sociable character and the conversational aptitude innate in the French encountered the milieu of the drawing-room manners and the moment of oratorical analysis. The opposite effect came about in seventeenth-century England when the harsh and solitary English genius tried blunderingly to adopt the new-born politeness. The former resulted in the noble and regular literature under Louis XIV, the latter in "the imperfect literature, the scandalous comedy, the abortive drama under Dryden and Wycherley."[9] André Chevrillon explains the geometrical relationship among the three forces in this way: "The national spirit describes a curve that is unforeseeable because two of the forces shaping it are variables; yet in that part of it which is drawn its elements are revealed in the light of history. The first element (race) of the entire curve remains constant, but at each point race is affected by the action of the other two elements, so that one sees but one movement."[10]

Although Taine was not the first critic who established a relationship between literature and history,[11] none before him had brought such a formidable array of method and knowledge to bear upon this subject; moreover, the effort in the past had been to provide a better explanation of the literary work by placing it in its historical context. Taine's announced goal reverses this relationship: "Given a literature, a philosophy, a society, an art, a group of arts, what is the moral condition which produced it? What are the conditions of race, milieu, moment most fitted to produce this moral condition?"[12] The answer to this problem, illustrated through great men, had necessarily to be selective, not only in the choice of writers but in the aspects emphasized in the writer's work. Consequently it is misdirected criticism to reproach Taine for incompleteness[13] or especially for his failure to explain why a particular great writer was a genius.

IV   *Taine on Genius and Great Writers*

Not that Taine did not have definite ideas on genius. As in his philosophical writings, he insisted that genius is not a mysterious phenomenon come out of nowhere but the effect of discoverable causes and favorable circumstances. "Genius is nothing but a developed power, and no power can develop fully except in the country where it is naturally encountered and in everybody, where education nourishes it, example fortifies it, character supports it, and the public brings it out."[14] The number of children who are potential geniuses is probably the same at all times; only at some times the surrounding climate is favorable and more reach full bloom, while at other times it is unfavorable with corresponding results.

A related criticism frequently directed at Taine's Introduction to the *History of English Literature* complains that race, milieu and moment do not explain why X was a great writer and his brother, who was subject to the same influences, turned out to be a minor author or a nonentity. One answer to this recurring objection lies in the master faculty, as previously pointed out. Yet, in the Introduction Taine has little to say about that important function, probably because he is dealing there not with individuals but with races and nations; however, a mere perusal of the five volumes will reveal the use he makes of master faculty in analyzing individual authors.

From the very beginning of his career as a critic Taine had drawn a sharp distinction between what we can know about an author and what we cannot claim to know. Writing about the

French historian Michelet, he states that history "rejects those foolhardy suppositions which explain in advance and in a peremptory manner the character of Maximilian, of Charles V and so many others by combining the qualities of the five or six races which produced their ancestors. The historians ought to learn from the natural scientists that this sort of laws concerning species, valid when one deals with great multitudes, are extremely dubious when it comes to individuals, and that one risks having one's judgment discredited by attributing to the cross-breeding of families all the actions and feelings of the men produced by this mixture."[15]

In a letter to Sainte-Beuve, written in reply to the first article on the *History of English Literature* by his colleague, Taine went still further in clarifying what he had already attempted to state in the Preface of his *Essays*: "Yes, analysis is powerless if we wish to represent completely and in all its shades the absolutely special, personal, infinitely complex and variable impression which constitutes a human character. But note that this difficulty is found everywhere, in an animal, a plant, or a shell. . . . No, analysis is not powerless if we merely seek to note the general characteristics which classify an individual among his genus and his species, if we mark the generative and regulating forces of his actions, and if we indicate the degree of these forces. I have attempted to depict individuals in my book: Bunyan, Shakespeare, Byron, Fielding. They are none the less individuals even though belonging to a class, because a class is composed of individuals. They are not any less spontaneous for being regulated by general laws, because these laws operate through individuals."[16]

V   *Comparisons of French and English Authors*

The five volumes that make up Taine's *History of English Literature* were written for the French reading public. It is consequently only natural to find in this work constant comparisons with French literature. One would be tempted to assign this study to comparative literature if the comparisons were not usually employed to serve the particular view the author wants to advance. He does not compare English and French literature in order to point out what two authors have in common or how one literature influenced the other. Rather he uses one literature to underline weaknesses or strengths in the other. Molière and even Racine receive lavish praise when compared with English Restoration dramatists; George Sand illustrates how to depict passionate women as compared to Dickens' who are merely decent; Balzac is superior to Thackeray in presenting a fascinating portrayal of a wicked woman, and Musset, Taine's favorite poet, is frankly preferred to Tennyson. In this respect he continued previous views expressed by Mme. de Staël who, early in the century, had drawn a line between the literatures of the North and of the South, but again he goes beyond his predecessors by carrying his ideas to their ultimate consequences. Beneath the French and English he examines the characteristics of the Latin and Germanic races and from their inherent traits and milieu he derives the reasons for their actions and mentality.

We have already seen that the Latin race, living in a temperate climate, had the leisure necessary to become civilized and cultivate the fine arts. The Latins love conversation and sensuous pleasures; hence they demand constant refinements and novelty. As a result they easily turn into rhetoricians, dilettantes, epicureans or libertines. Quickly excited and flighty, their excessive talking tends to produce unstable governments. Intellectually, they like to analyze feelings and ideas, and they excel in the art of developing a line of reasoning, advancing step by step and linking their ideas by transitions. Esthetically, they prefer beautiful to strong expression, form to depth. "The literatures of Latin populations are classic and nearly or remotely allied to Greek poesy, Roman eloquence, the Italian renaissance, and the age of Louis XIV; they refine and ennoble, they embellish and prune, they systematize and give proportion. Their latest masterpiece is the drama of Racine, who is the painter of princely ways, court proprieties, social paragons, and cultivated natures; the master of an oratorical style, skilful composition and literary elegance."[17]

The members of the Germanic race exhibit quite different characteristics. The far harsher climate of their habitat and a half-civilized life have turned them inward and made them less susceptible to exterior elegance and refinements. Slower in their outward reactions, latent violence in them is accompanied by a vivid poetic imagination, a melancholic disposition and a sense of duty. Patient, hard-working, and capable of devoting themselves to long, arduous and boring tasks, they are superior to the Latins in erudition, philosophy, languages, laboratory research, the compilation of dictionaries, and in material accomplishments. Intellectually, they are capable of probing deeply, and their patience enables them to create organized and free governments. With the exception of Flanders, the Germanic nations, subordinating outward to inward worship and formal authority to personal convictions, embraced Protestantism. "The Germanic literatures, . . . are romantic; their primitive source is the Edda and the ancient sagas of the north; their greatest masterpiece is the drama of Shakespeare, that is to say the crude and complete representation of actual life, with all its atrocious, ignoble and common-place details, its sublime and brutal instincts, the entire outgrowth of human character displayed before us, now in a familiar style bordering on the trivial, and now poetic even to lyricism, always independent of rule, incoherent, excessive, but of an incomparable force, and filling our souls with the warm and palpitating passion of which it is the outcry."[18]

The basically different dispositions of the Latin and Germanic races lead to two kinds of mentalities which can best be illustrated by the way each reacts when faced with a whole and distinct object: a tree, an animal, a sentiment, or an event. Will it divide the object into its parts and stop at analysis, or can it go beyond analysis, seize the whole and reproduce it through an instructive and sympathetic effort?

All minds take one or other of these routes, and are divided by them into two great classes, corresponding to opposite temperaments. In the first are the plain men of science, the popularisers, orators, writers—in general, the classical ages and the Latin races; in the second are the poets, prophets, commonly the inventors—in general, the romantic ages and the Germanic races. The first proceed gradually from one idea to the next: they are methodical and cautious; they speak for the world at large, and prove what they say; they divide the field which they would traverse into sections to begin with, in order to exhaust their subject; they march straight and level roads, so as to be sure against a fall; they proceed by transitions, enumerations, summaries; they advance from general to still more general conclusions; they form the exact and complete classification of a group. When they go beyond simple analysis, their whole talent consists in eloquently pleading a thesis. Amongst the contemporaries of Carlyle, Macaulay is the most complete model of this species of mind. The others, after having violently and confusedly rummaged amongst the details of a group, plunge with a sudden spring into the mother-notion. They see it then in its entirety; they perceive the powers which organise it; they reproduce it by divination; they depict it in miniature by the most expressive words, the strongest ideas; they are not capable of decomposing it into regular series, they always perceive it in a lump. They think only by sudden concentrations of vehement ideas. They have a vision of distant effects or living actions; they are revealers or poets. Michelet, amongst the French, is the best example of this form of intellect, and Carlyle is an English Michelet.[19]

VI *Shakespeare*

We understand now why Shakespeare is at the center of Taine's work, not only as England's greatest writer, not only as the one who most perfectly illustrates Taine's view of human nature, but, in a class by himself, as the ideal model of the Germanic mentality. Indeed, it can be said that the *History of English Literature* is both an attack on Classicism and a hymn to Shakespeare, the high mark to whom all preceding English literature points, the perfect author, who provides a touchstone by which lesser men are measured and on which they come to shipwreck. How could even a Samuel Richardson or a Fielding[20] stand comparison with a genius whose master faculty was complete and passionate imagination, one who could see the whole with all its parts in one powerful glance?

Picture yourself . . . the complete idea, that is, an inner representation, so abundant and full, that it exhausts all the properties and relations of the object, all its inward and outward aspects; that it exhausts them instantaneously; that it conceives of the animal all at once, its colour, the play of the light upon its skin, its form, the quivering of its outstretched limbs, the flash of its eyes, and at the same time its passion of the moment, its excitement, its dash; and beyond this its instincts, their composition, their causes, their history; so that the hundred thousand characteristics which make up its condition and its nature find their analogues in the imagination which concentrates and reflects them: there you have the artist's conception, the poet's—Shakespeare's; so superior to that of the logician, of the mere savant or man of the world, the only one capable of penetrating to the basis of things, of extricating the inner from beneath the outer man, of feeling through sympathy, and imitating without effort, the disorderly roundabout of human imaginations and impressions, of reproducing life with its infinite fluctuations, its apparent contradictions, its concealed logic; in short, to create as nature creates.[21]

Shakespeare owes his exalted position in Taine's hierarchy of authors to other qualities as well. Not only English writers are measured against his achievements but also French Classicism and its representatives. Assuming the Romantic stance which places Shakespeare above Racine, espoused, among others, by his model Stendhal in *Racine et Shakespeare* (1823), Taine presents arguments which, however arguable, repose on a firmer and more consistent basis than those of his predecessors. By stressing the differences which separate Shakespeare's view of man and of the world from that of French Classicism, Taine gives expression to his own psychological convictions which see man not as a rational being but as precariously tottering at the edge of madness, just fortunate enough to be assailed by hallucinations which usually turn out to correspond to reality:

Shakespeare lets justness and clearness look out for themselves, and attains life. From amidst his complex conception and his coloured semi-vision he grasps a fragment, a quivering fibre, and shows it; it is for you, from this fragment, to divine the rest. He, behind the word, has a whole picture, an attitude, a long argument abridged, a mass of swarming ideas; you know them, these abbreviative, condensive words: these are they which we launch out from the furnace of invention, in a fit of passion: words of slang or of fashion, which appeal to local memory or individual experience; little concocted and incorrect phrases, which, by their irregularity, express the suddenness and the breaks of the inner sensation; trivial words, exaggerated figures. There is a gesture beneath each, a quick contraction of the brows, a curl of laughing lips, a clown's trick, an unhinging of the whole machine. None of them mark ideas; each is the extremity and issue of a complete mimic action; none is the expression and definition of a partial and limited idea. This is why Shakespeare is strange and powerful, obscure and original, beyond all the poets of his or any other age; the most immoderate of all violators of language, the most marvelous of all creators of souls, the farthest removed from regular logic and classical reason, the one most capable of exciting in us a world of forms, and of placing living beings before us. . . .

If Shakespeare had framed a psychology, he would have said . . .: Man is a nervous machine, governed by a mood, disposed to hallucinations, transported by unbridled passions, essentially unreasoning, a mixture of animal and poet, having no rapture but mind, no sensibility but virtue, imagination for prompter and guide, and led at random, by the most determinate and complex circumstances, to pain, crime, madness and death.[22]

John S. White was justified in claiming that "no other Latin experienced Shakespeare so profoundly as Taine,"[23] for when the critic speaks of the ideal author he is completely engrossed in his subject which makes for a less perfect illustration of his method but, in return, for some of the finest pages he ever penned. To describe Shakespeare's comedies, Taine compares French and English wit: "One, altogether French, which is but reason, a foe to paradox, scorner of folly, a sort of incisive common sense, having no occupation but to render truth amusing and evident, the most effective weapon with an intelligent and vain people; such was the wit of Voltaire and the drawing rooms. The other, that of improvisators and artists, is a mere inventive transport, paradoxical, unshackled, exuberant, a sort of self-entertainment, a phantasmagoria of images, quibbles, strange ideas, dazing and intoxicating, like the movement and illumination of a ball. Such is the wit of Mercutio, of the clowns, of Beatrice, Rosalind, and Benedick. They laugh, not from a sense of the ridiculous, but from the desire to laugh. You must look elsewhere for the campaigns which aggressive reason makes against human folly. Here folly is in its full bloom. Our folk think of amusement, and nothing more."[24]

But soon, leaving all comparisons aside, Taine applies his own psychological insights to the study of Hamlet in whom he sees a reflection of Shakespeare himself. While this interpretation is not new, Taine's conception of man made him applaud Shakespeare's character as illustrating his own "brink-of-madness" view of human conduct. A personage with a delicate soul and impassioned imagination, Hamlet already shows signs of approaching monomania in the contortions of thoughts and latent hallucinations contained in his first monologues, but when the Ghost asks him to swear, the last dams of sanity give way.

Understand that as he says that his teeth chatter, "pale as his shirt, his knees knocking each other." Intense anguish ends with a burst of laughter, which is nothing else than a spasm. Thenceforth Hamlet speaks as though he had a continuous nervous attack. His madness is feigned, I admit; but his mind, as a door whose hinges are twisted, swings and bangs to every wind with a mad precipitance and with a discordant noise. He has no need to search for the strange ideas, apparent incoherencies, exaggerations, the deluge of sarcasms which he accumulates. He finds them within him; he does himself no violence, he simply gives himself up to them. . . .

He is not master of his acts; occasion dictates them; he cannot plan a murder, but must improvise it. A too lively imagination exhausts energy, by the accumulation of images and by the fury of intentness which absorbs it. You recognise in him a poet's soul, made not to act, but to dream, which is lost in contemplating the phantoms of its creation, which sees the imaginary world too clearly to play a part in the real world; an artist whom evil chance has made a prince, whom worse chance has made an avenger of crime, and who, destined by nature for genius, is condemned by fortune to madness and unhappiness. Hamlet is Shakespeare, and, at the close of this gallery of portraits which have all some features of his own, Shakespeare has painted himself in the most striking of all.[25]

VII *Individual Authors and Periods*

As in his previous literary criticism Taine remains severe on those who fall into the Classical mold. Ben Jonson, hampered by his logical mind and preoccupied with Classical rules, had difficulties in creating living characters and was saved only by those qualities he shared with his race and his age: a sense of the natural and of life, the exact knowledge of details, and his ability to deal frankly with frank passions.[26] While the Renaissance signaled the rebirth of the Saxon genius in English literature, the Restoration created a crisis by warping the development of English society and literature, and Taine cannot find enough contempt to heap on this epoch. Racine is showered with praise by him when compared to Otway or Wycherley;[27] and Pope, despite occasional tips of the hat, is finally dismissed as boring.[28] The popularity of Samuel Johnson during the Restoration places Taine before an almost insoluble riddle that can in the end only be explained by the character of the English reader:

We wish to know what ideas have made him popular. Here the astonishment of the Frenchman redoubles. We vainly turn over the pages of his *Dictionary,* his eight volumes of essays, his ten volumes of biographies, his numberless articles, his conversation so carefully collected; we yawn. His truths are too true; we already knew his precepts by heart. We learn from him that life is short, and we ought to improve the few moments accorded to us; that a mother ought not to bring up her son as a dandy; that a man ought to repent of his crimes, and yet avoid superstition; that in everything we ought to be active, and not hurried. We thank him for these sage counsels, but we mutter to ourselves that we could have done very well without them. We should like to know who could have been the lovers of *ennui* who have bought up thirteen thousand copies. We then remember that sermons are liked in England, and that these *Essays* are sermons. We discover that men of reflection do not need bold or striking ideas, but palpable and profitable truths. They demand to be furnished with a useful provision of authentic documents on man and his existence, and demand nothing more.[29]

With the advent of the nineteenth century Taine finds the English at their best again. If Shakespeare occupies a place apart in his admiration, the critic feels personally closest, among the English authors, to Macaulay and Byron who represent his Classical bent of mind and his Romantic ideal, respectively. The former he admired so greatly as to take for his own the title of his *Critical and Historical Essays*; in the latter he praises the greatest and most English of all writers whose spirit of poetic and rebellious imagination recalls "that somber madness which urged forward the Scandinavian Berserkers, when, in an open bark, under a sky cloven with lightning, they launched out upon the tempest, whose fury they had breathed."[30]

"A Scald transplanted into modern life, who in this over-well regulated world did not find his vocation,"[31] Byron fought against his situation and declared war on society. For lack of action he had dreams. This is why he would have been an excellent pamphleteer and, although he became a poet, he wrote in his own fashion. Adopting the Classical system, he pleads his passion and, in fact, practically never transcends his own self. If we compare Goethe's *Faust* and Byron's *Manfred*, the difference between the German and the English character becomes apparent. The former deals with metaphysical problems and depicts a universal personage; the latter, owing to the English traits of being concerned with practical and moral matters, cares little about the supernatural, for his energetic will and courage flinch before nothing. In Manfred, Childe Harold, Lara, the Giaour and the rest of his heroes, Byron portrays not the universal but the individual, specifically himself. Hence he does not invent but observe; he does not create, he describes. In the same manner he is not interested in history and nature in order to understand them or forget himself before them; instead, he seeks in them and impresses upon them his own passions. In Byron the author salutes the most distinguished prey of the malady of the age by acknowledging the deep imprint Romanticism has left on his own. "Our generation, like the preceding, has been tainted by the malady of the age, and will never be more than half be quit of it. We shall arrive at truth, not at calm. All we can heal at present is our intellect; we have no hold upon our sentiments."[32]

One of the most un-English thinkers is Carlyle whom Taine appreciated nonetheless because he had introduced German philosophy in England, but his greatest favorite among contemporary thinkers was Stuart Mill. In a page that shows him a master of delicate description Taine mingles man and milieu, balanced, practical mentality and age-old traditions as he reports his discussion with a disciple of Mill at Oxford on an August morning:

The architecture of all ages had mingled their ogives, trefoils, statues, and columns; time had softened their tints; the sun united them in its light, and the old city seemed a shrine to which every age and every genius had successively added a jewel. Beyond this, the river rolled its broad sheets of silver; the mowers stood up to the knee in the high grass of the meadows. Myriads of buttercups and meadow-sweet grasses, bending under the weight of their grey heads, plants sated with the dew of the night, swarmed in the rich soil. Words cannot express this freshness of tints, and their luxuriance of vegetation. . . . Around, as though to guard them, enormous trees, four centuries old, extended in regular lines; and I found in them a new trace of that practical good sense which has effected revolutions without committing ravages; which, while reforming in all directions, has destroyed nothing; which has preserved both its trees and its constitution, which has lopped off the dead branches without levelling the trunk; which alone, in our days, among nations, is in the enjoyment not only of the present, but of the past.[33]

Throughout the *History of English Literature* Taine applies his technique of individual analysis by means of master faculty and of summary by memorable phrases. Sir Walter Scott was "the Homer of modern citizen life," Wordsworth, "an essentially moral philosopher, and an excessively sensitive man"; Dickens is characterized by impassioned sensibility. In spite of his admiration for the famous English novelist, Taine depicts him at one point as "a man who, with a stewpan in one hand and a postillon's whip in the other, took to making prophecies."[34] The critic never forgets his basic purpose, which is to show the English character through its literature. He therefore links Dickens' protest against society's treatment of the weak to the sentiments that stir deep in the English soul in spite of practical faculties and a positive mind fashioned by the milieu of an insular position, the necessity of commerce, and the abundant possession of raw material: "We do not believe that this contrast between the weak and the strong, or this outcry against society in favour of nature, are the caprice of an artist or the chance of the moment. When we penetrate deeply into the history of English genius, we find that its primitive foundation was impassioned sensibility, and that its natural expression was lyrical exaltation. . . . The social man has not destroyed the natural man. This frozen crust, this unsociable pride, this rigid attitude, often cover a good and tender being. It is the English mask of a German head; and when a talented writer, often a writer of genius, reaches the sensibility which is bruised or buried by education and national institutions, he moves his reader in the most inner depths, and becomes the master of all hearts."[35]

In part Taine's intention in his *History of English Literature* was no doubt to use the English in order to criticize the French the way Stendhal had opposed Italian passion and spontaneity to French materialism and stuffiness. But as he advanced in his study of the English character, he became increasingly irritated at British preoccupation with morality, a concern he considered harmful both because it leads to hypocrisy and because it forces authors into a false portrayal of human beings:

It is therefore to misunderstand man, to reduce him, as Thackeray and English literature generally do, to an aggregate of virtues and vices; it is to lose sight in him of all but the exterior and social side; it is to neglect the inner and natural element. You will find the same fault in English criticism, always moral, never psychological, bent on exactly measuring the degree of human honesty, ignorant of the mechanism of our sentiments and faculties; you will find the same fault in English religion, which is but an emotion or a discipline; in their philosophy, destitute of metaphysics; and if you ascend to the source, according to the rule which derives vices from virtues, and virtues from vices, you

will see all these weaknesses derived from their native energy, their
practical education, and that sort of severe and religious poetic instinct
which has in time past made them protestant and Puritan.[36]

VIII   *How Taine Applied His Theory*

Were the *History of English Literature* no more than a collection
of separate essays, such as the last-added volume on contemporary
authors, then it would merely testify to the critic's good or bad
taste, his personal perceptiveness and his vivid style. What makes
this work unique is its demonstration that a history of literature
can be a study in the continuity of a race and of changing social
and intellectual conditions as well.

Starting with the premise that "beneath every literature there is
a philosophy. Beneath every work of art there is an idea of nature
and of life. Whether the author knows it or not, he writes in order
to exhibit it,"[37] Taine calls on his formidable grasp of art and
history, on the reigning personage, to illuminate an entire epoch
and to indicate transitions to the next one. Long before Huizinga,[38]
the French critic illustrated through art the waning of the Middle
Ages:

When you look at a cathedral of that time, you feel a sort of fear.
Substance is wanting; the walls are hollowed out to make room for
windows, the elaborate work of the porches, the wonderful growth of
the slender columns, the thin curvature of arches—everything seems to
totter; support has been withdrawn to give way to ornament. Without
external prop or buttress, and artificial aid of iron clamp-work, the
building would have crumbled to pieces on the first day: as it is, it
undoes itself; we have to maintain on the spot a colony of masons
continually to ward off the continual decay. But our eyes lose themselves in following the wavings and twistings of the endless fretwork;
the dazzling centrerose of the portal and the painted glass throw a
diapered light on the carved stalls of the choir, the gold-work of the
altar, the long array of damascened and glittering copes, the crowd of
statues, gradually rising; and amid this violet light, this quivering purple, amid these arrows of gold which pierce the gloom, the building is
like the tail of a mystical peacock. So most of the poems of the time
are barren of foundation; at most a trite morality serves them for
main-stay: in short, the poet thought of nothing else than spreading
out before us a glow of colours and a jumble of forms.[39]

Of the new spirit which announces the Renaissance, Taine writes with the penetration that distinguished the famous work of Burkhardt, his contemporary. A changed situation due to peace and better economic conditions caused people to look at the world around them differently:

It seems as though men had suddenly opened their eyes, and seen. In fact, they attain a new and superior kind of intelligence. It is the proper feature of this age, that men no longer make themselves masters of objects by bits, or isolated, or through scholastic or mechanical classifications, but as a whole, in general and complete views, with the eager grasp of a sympathetic spirit, which, being placed before a vast object, penetrates it in all its parts. . . . An extraordinary warmth of soul, a superabundant and splendid imagination, reveries, visions, artists, believers, founders, creators—that is what such a form of intellect produces; for to create we must have, as had Luther and Loyola, Michael Angelo and Shakespeare, an idea, not abstract, partial and dry, but well defined, finished, sensible—a true creation, which acts inwardly, and struggles to appear to the light. This was Europe's grand age, and the most notable epoch of human growth. To this day we live from its sap, we only carry on its pressure and efforts.[40]

This new spirit is once more illustrated through a new reigning model and a new art: "The ideal to which all efforts were turning, on which all thoughts depended, and which completely raised this civilization, was the strong and happy man, fortified by all powers to accomplish his wishes, and disposed to use them in pursuit of his happiness. If you would see this idea in its grandest operation, you must seek it in the arts, such as Italy made them and carried throughout Europe. . . . The new Jesus is a 'crucified Jupiter,' as Pulci called him; the Virgins which Raphael designed naked, before covering them with garments, are beautiful girls, quite earthly, relatives of the Fornarina. The saints which Michael Angelo arranges and contorts in heaven on the judgment-day are an assembly of athletes, capable of fighting well and daring much."[41]

The admirable thing about the *History of English Literature* is that, despite legitimate objections which may be raised about his judgment of individual authors, Taine nonetheless fulfilled the ambitious promise he made at the outset, namely to arrive at a definition of the English character through its literature by bringing to bear on it the factors of race, milieu and moment in the course of changing times. The *History of English Literature* is Taine's greatest work of literary criticism and, along with his pioneer articles on Balzac and Stendhal, ranks among the monuments of French literary criticism of the nineteenth century. For one hundred years critics and students alike have mouthed his formulas of master faculty, the reigning model, the writer as expression of his times and the tripartite theory of race, milieu and moment in a mechanical way without realizing that, like all general formulas, these are capable of changing with the times. As scientific knowledge increases, so these terms take on new meanings; as instruments of observation are perfected, so the equations become more complex. It is the task of Taine's successors not to criticize inevitable oversimplifications but to adjust his terms to correspond to current data. Thus, if our concept of race has changed, if we should discover the definite relationship between heredity and environment, Taine's terms will have to be brought up-to-date. Yet, while it may turn out that the weight assigned to each factor needs to be shifted, the formula expressing their interrelationship is thereby not necessarily invalidated.

Like all methods, Taine's has inherent limitations and omissions. Since it attempts to seize the author in his permanent traits, little attention is given to the evolution he undergoes during his artistic career. In addition, because of its historical orientation, the method can be applied with more likelihood of success to past than to contemporary authors. Finally, the assertion that great writers are representatives of their time stands up in most cases, but again the formula needs to be expanded. The very writers Taine counted among his favorites, Stendhal and Byron, prove that an author may write in opposition to his time, so that the formula should state that great writers express the spirit of their epoch directly or negatively. Taine's insistence that the work of an author who is not in harmony with his times will not come to fruition raises considerable problems. The formula may have fitted the literary situation in France prior to the Revolution, even though during that time too a writer sometimes was at least out-of-pace with his epoch, so that his ideas were accepted only much later (Descartes, for example), but it is evident that the divorce between artist and public has been widening considerably since the nineteenth century. So great has the cleavage become that Albert Camus, in his acceptance speech of the 1957 Nobel Prize for Literature, could claim that in the past one hundred fifty years a literature of revolt has developed and that the best works created have been written against the society of the time.[42]

If Taine's formula were sufficient, the bestseller list would be a perfect means of gauging an author's importance and greatness. But the low sale of Stendhal's novels during his lifetime, his belated recognition, the severe judgment of posterity on artists most popular during their time, the likelihood that there is mutual influence between the writer and his time,[43] make it clear that this is not a one-to-one relationship. Still, Taine's approach remains effective when dealing with long periods (the Middle Ages, the Renaissance, the Classical period) or in his treatment of the history of English literature.

Since this examination of Taine's literary criticism was primarily designed to illustrate his method, little has been said of his esthetic opinions. Although, in his literary criticism, these are assigned a minor role, he never neglects them altogether; in fact, he frequently deals with style, but rarely for its own sake, his purpose usually being to illustrate through it changing modes of thought. Esthetic considerations will assume a greater importance as Taine turns to the field of art where his method, perfected by experience in literature, was to prove that it could be extended to new objects and meet new problems and challenges.

CHAPTER 5

The Art Critic

"What I perceive through a work of art, as through any work, is the state of mind which produced it."[1] This declaration of principle could serve as a motto for all of Taine's criticism but especially for the *Philosophy of Art,* translated into English as *Lectures on Art.*[2] In his *History of English Literature* he had attempted to discover the English spirit through the literature of that nation; in the *Lectures on Art* he turns to new problems. What is a work of art? Which are the conditions necessary and favorable for the production of great works of art? Are all artistic creations of equal value or are some superior to others? Is morality a legitimate factor in artistic judgment?

Once again the critic was not writing a history of art but using typical examples drawn from art in Italy, the Netherlands, and Greece to supply illustrated answers to his questions. Nor did he limit himself to painting; sculpture, literature, architecture and music are also called upon to typify a particular atmosphere or age. Jean-François Revel[3] felicitously calls him a psychologist of culture who makes us understand works of art by explaining how they came about, to what needs of the time they correspond and how they were viewed by the contemporaries of the artist.

Taine's method remains basically the same. Race, milieu, moment, intellectual climate, the reigning character, all these reappear, but because of the nature of the work, milieu and intellectual climate tend to predominate while the master faculty scarcely makes an appearance. The new elements which deal with value differentiations are somewhat unexpected in a scientific critic who previously had excluded all moral judgments from his considerations. Thus the *Lectures on Art* go far beyond the *History of Eng-*

lish Literature, for here Taine no longer studies one single country but art as a whole in Western culture. In these lectures to an enthusiastic class of art students we find the summing up of Taine's critical views, for it will be his last important work in the field of criticism.

I   *The Artist and His Time*

Leaving aside for the time being architecture and music, Taine finds that the remaining arts (poetry, sculpture and painting) seem to share one trait: the imitation of a living model. The careers of the great artists prove this point, for they can be divided into youth and maturity, during which time the creator keeps his eyes fixed on nature, and decadence when, feeling there is nothing new to discover, he uses his know-how to fabricate an artificial work of art. Yet if minute imitation were the desired result, the artist could not compete with photography. Michelangelo exaggerated the trunk and muscles of his statues on the tomb of the Medicis to express his despair at the tyranny and injustice in his country; and Rubens illustrated the new abundance and prosperity of his time by depicting enlarged members, rosy flesh and orgies in his *Kermesse.* Therefore "the end of a work of art is to manifest some essential or salient character, consequently some important idea, clearer and more completely than is attainable from real objects. Art accomplishes this end by employing a group of connected parts, the relationships of which it systematically modifies. In the three imitative arts of sculpture, painting, and poetry, these groups correspond to real objects."[4]

Next Taine turns to one of his favorite principles: the "inevitable and fixed" relationship between a work of art and the general state of mind and the surrounding conditions which determine it. A particular work of art is not an isolated phenomenon but forms an integral part of the artist's entire production which, in turn, is related to an artistic family, school or movement which, finally, is determined by the state of mind and manners of the times. The process operates in this way. A moral climate exists at a given time. This may be one of melancholy, joyfulness, or some intermediate state due to the surrounding circumstances (political, economic, etc.) which, in turn, create in people corresponding aptitudes, needs, and particular feelings. These may be warlike or gentle predispositions, a need for physical activity or for sedate conversations in drawing rooms. From these aptitudes, needs, and feelings springs the representative character,[5] that is, a model character admired by his contemporaries. This model character is either both depicted and appealed to in works of the imitative arts or else, as in music and architecture, they are addressed to him.

To illustrate his point Taine uses the example of the circumstances necessary to make seeds develop into an orange tree: the proper soil, a favorable climate, the absence of other plants that might inhibit its growth. As the orange tree requires a *physical* temperature to grow, so the artist, a human seed which nature produces in almost unvarying quantities at all times, needs the proper *moral* temperature in order to develop fully. Consequently an artist producing sad works in a happy moral climate or joyful works during unhappy times is as unlikely to succeed and to be accepted as an orange tree may be expected to grow in Siberia.

As usual, Taine's formula is attractive in its close linking of the natural and human sciences, but its insistence on the unvarying relationship between the individual artist and the reigning mood of the time needs some modification. We have already had occasion to cite the example of Stendhal who wrote in opposition to the prevailing conditions in France in the 1830's, who encountered indeed little appreciation during his lifetime but was awarded posthumous glory some fifteen years after his death—by Taine himself! It is not difficult to discover judgments on individual artists in Taine's very works that would contradict this rigid one-to-one relationship. Thus Leonardo da Vinci was "a completely modern man, at an infinite distance from his century; through him the Renaissance touches our time without transition."[6] Of Giotto, Taine remarks: "Although born in a mystical century, he is not mystical and even though Dante's friend, he does not resemble him."[7] These great creators may very well be exceptions and Taine's general formula may still be valid for the majority of cases, yet these very exceptions force us to modify the rigidity of the formula.

A similar, and somewhat more serious objection may be raised against the critic's dictum that the public will only welcome those artistic productions which correspond to its state of mind. In two successive paragraphs Taine both exposes his principle and then illustrates it by an apparent contradiction. After describing the turbulent life in Renaissance Italy, he continues:

The more a man has suffered, dreaded or grieved, the more delighted he is to expand. The more his soul has been beset with painful anxieties or with dark thoughts, the greater his pleasure in the presence of harmonious and noble beauty. The more he has strained or bridled himself either for action or for dissimulation, the more he enjoys when he is able to give vent to and unbend himself. A calm, blooming Madonna in his alcove, the shape of a valiant youth over his dresser, occupies his eye the more agreeably after tragic preoccupations and funereal reveries. Pleasant, earnest, complex conversation, incessantly renewed and varied, does not exist there for his relief; in the silence in which he shuts himself up he discourses inwardly with forms and colors; while the usual solemnity of his life, the multitude of his perils and the obstacles in the way of his expansiveness only contribute to intensifying and refining the impressions which he derives from the arts.[8]

If it is true that a man who has been experiencing tensions, excitement and danger in his public life craves calmness, harmony and silence, then one is justified in extending this observation to claiming that people who encounter sad and depressing conditions all day long would prefer more joyful and optimistic works for their private pleasure. And what is true for individuals might also apply to entire intellectual movements. It is surprising that Taine, steeped as he was in Hegel's philosophy, failed to take into account the German thinker's dialectical approach in describing the effects exerted on art by the spirit of the times and the reigning model. These two, by their very dominance, call into being their antitheses, in the form either of caricature or of completely contrary manifestations, until the two movements blend into a new synthesis. Dialectical considerations would have lent a greater sense of complexity to Taine's monolithic manner of viewing historical periods.

II   *Conditions for Great Artistic Epochs*

The most valuable part of Taine's theoretical views on art lies in his research of the conditions that permit and bring about a flowering of the arts. Just as for Taine sanity is a precarious state, just as an orange tree needs the confluence of favorable conditions to produce its fruit, so a number of widely separated factors must be simultaneously present in order that a great artistic period may result. These prerequisites consist of: *(1)* a certain level of civilization already attained; *(2)* an economic and intellectual situation that encourages the production of art; *(3)* aptitudes and tastes shared by artist and public alike; *(4)* an art that maintains its national traits; and *(5)* a vigorous, energetic nation.

Three conditions are necessary to enable man to produce and appreciate great art. First, he must be cultivated, i.e., he must have left behind him the primitive state of barbarianism and oppression, enjoy a reasonable amount of leisure and crave noble and refined pleasures. Next, there must be present an aptitude for spontaneous images, one that is neither smothered under nor mutilated by ideas which deform the primitive vision, so that word and image arise simultaneously in the mind of the artist. Finally, experiences, habits and passions must be such as to induce artists to use the human body as their principal subject with a preference for sane, strong and active figures.

Art flourishes best in times of prosperity, provided the mind is not kept enslaved to ideas determined by authority. Thus the English and Flemish Renaissance coincided with the end of wars, the improvement of the general well-being and the relaxation of religious restraints. It is at such periods of transition, between times of heroic and epicurean manners, that art, partaking of both, achieves that delicate moment of magnificence which Italy experienced between the fifteenth and sixteenth centuries. On the other hand, the inadequate fusion of two tendencies, the old notion of the divine world and the new one of the natural world, accounts for the failure of Italian painting in the fourteenth century as illustrated by Pietro d'Orvieto's Christ who, except for his head and feet, disappears almost completely under an immense disc symbolizing the shape of the world and the spheres rolling into each other.

These conditions in themselves present of course no guarantee for the creation of great artistic works. It takes artists and an appreciative public to turn favorable circumstances into creative periods of high art. "It has been remarked that two conditions are essential for the production of great works; the first one is the vivacity of a spontaneous sentiment, personal and characteristic, expressed according as the feeling arises, without the fear of any restraint or subject to any direction; the second is the presence of sympathetic souls, the outward and steady support of kindred ideas, through which the vague ideas we carry about with us are gestated, nourished, perfected, multiplied and strengthened."[9]

To be valid art must be national. Taine had already shown in his *History of English Literature* that English Restoration works failed in their attempt to make their own what was essentially foreign, namely French Classicism. The same setback results when, during the last seventy-five years of the sixteenth century, the Flemish painters try to assimilate the Italian style. The two essential traits of Italian artists, their depiction of the natural, sane human body and their habit of simplifying by embellishing to represent general and not individual man, are both alien to the Flemish artists. Living in a cold and humid country, they are not accustomed to seeing well-proportioned bodies and, being of a Germanic race, their moral scruples keep them from accepting the pagan idea of nudity. At the same time their realistic vision concentrates not on man in general but assigns importance to his peculiarities. Subjecting themselves to a discipline so contrary to their natural inclinations, Jan de Mabuse, Bernard Van Orley, Lambert Lombard, Franz Floris, Martin de Vos and their fellow "Italians" seem like people who speak only Italian but with an accent and with flagrant mistakes.

A great artistic age depends very closely on the active energies of the entire nation and comes to an end at the same time as the country loses its vitality. After a period of splendor, the Dutch begin to show signs of weakening about 1667 after suffering defeats. Growing soft from excessive prosperity, the heroes become bourgeois, as can be seen from the rich interiors painted by Terburg and Metzu. In 1669 Rembrandt dies poor and ignored. When Louis XIV invades the country in 1672 he finds almost no resistance. Until the end of the seventeenth century masterworks continue to be produced, as a popular revolution keeps the national spirit alive, but after 1715 Holland becomes subject to invasions and humiliations, and painting loses its verve and becomes reduced to the flower paintings of De Witt, Rachel Ruysch and Van Huysum.

III *Art in Italy*

"Take away six lines at the beginning and six lines at the end, and M. Taine's volume, far from giving us a philosophy of art in Greece, will contain neither a word of art nor of philosophy."[10] This criticism by Edmond Scherer, although severe, may be applied to Taine's treatment of art in Italy and the Netherlands as well, if the reader expects to find descriptions and analyses of individual paintings or sculptures in the book. But since the author was far more concerned with the conditions required for the production of works of art, "philosophy" here must be taken to mean not the theoretical views of philosophers but the general state of mind, i.e. a collective philosophy which underlies the works of art produced during a given period.[11] If his students wished to read his impressions of Italian paintings, they merely had to consult his travel book on Italy, which forms indeed an indispensable companion to the *Philosophy of Art in Italy*.

There are definite flaws in Taine's treatment of art in Italy. For one thing, he is so anxious to involve the reader in the spirit of the Italian Renaissance that he piles anecdote upon anecdote; for another, he takes Benvenuto Cellini, often an unreliable witness, as his narrator. But when it comes to a general description of the milieu, of race, of state of mind, Taine is again in his real element. He depicts a state of affairs in which, for lack of habitual peace, of equitable justice and a watchful police, anxiety, violence and disorder reign over a race endowed with rhythmic and figurative imagination which attains modern culture while keeping feudal customs, joins energetic instincts with refined ideas and thinks in terms of sensible shapes.

Several additional factors contribute to the flowering of the arts at that particular time. The Italians, characterized by an extremely acute and quick mind that attains civilization almost effortlessly, enjoyed the advantage of not having been Teutonized, as other European countries, by the barbarian invasions. Consequently, and in Taine's theory this is of capital importance, in Italy images were not effaced by ideas. Rather, a balanced state resulted which, along with a concentration on the human body, enabled the artists to transfer to their canvases the colorful life they were witnessing: "A picturesque state of mind, that is to say, mid-way between pure ideas and pure images, energetic characters and passionate habits suited to giving a knowledge of and taste for beautiful physical forms, constitute the temporary circumstances which, added to the innate aptitudes of the race, produced in Italy, the great and perfect painting of the human form. We have, now, only to descend into the streets, or to enter the studios, and we shall see it giving itself birth. . . . The men of this day are amateurs of painting, not for an hour, for a single moment in their life, but throughout their life, in their religious ceremonies, in their national festivities, in their public receptions, in their avocations and in their amusements."[12]

By comparison with this fortunate combination of ingredients in Italy, we can now determine why elsewhere, despite generally favorable conditions, an equally successful artistic achievement failed to materialize. In Germany, the country of metaphysics and of philosophical systems, the preponderance of ideas prevents painters from expressing themselves through spontaneous images. In England the importance attached to material life and moral questions relegates painting to an inferior occupation practiced on an unnatural soil by artists incapable of balancing sensations and images. Even in France, where artistic productions surpass those of its neighbors, the excellence of Renaissance Italy has not been equalled. The principal reason for this is that French painting has tried to compete with literature, which resulted in works that are poetic, historical and dramatic rather than picturesque, in the sense in which Taine uses this term. Besides, in modern times so many luxuries have come to be considered indispensable, towns have grown to such enormous size, and modern democracies have opened up so many opportunities for previously unthought-of ambitions that mental energies are necessarily diverted to matters other than art.

IV *Art in Greece*

It should by now be apparent why Greek art corresponds to Taine's ideal. A simple life limited to the bare necessities, a beautiful country, a temperate climate, a religion without mystery, institutions designed to serve the purpose of the people and not vice versa—these features of Greek civilization might lead to a lack of grandeur in their religious conceptions but in turn permitted a concentration on the present life, all the more so since leisure provided opportunities for philosophical and artistic discussions in relatively small communities. Yet all these advantages would not

necessarily have insured the creation of great masterworks if it had
not been for favorable racial traits:

Delicacy of perception, an aptitude at seizing nice relationships, the
sense of gradation, is what allows the artist to construct a totality of
forms, colors, sounds and incidents, in short, elements and details, so
closely united among themselves by inward dependencies, that their
organization constitutes a living thing, surpassing in the imaginary
world the profound harmony of the actual world. The necessity of
clearness, a feeling for proportion, dislike of the vague and the abstract, contempt for the monstrous and exaggerated, and a taste for
accurate and defined contours, is what leads him to give his conceptions a shape which the imagination and senses can easily grasp, and,
consequently, to execute works comprehensible to every race and all
ages, and which, being human, are eternal. The love and worship of
this life, the sentiment of human energy and the necessity of calmness
and gayety, is what leads him to avoid depicting physical infirmity and
moral ills, to represent the health of the spirit and perfection of the
body, and to complete the acquired beauty of expression by the fundamental beauty of the subject. These are the distinct traits of their
entire art.[13]

The Greeks, moreover, reveal attitudes which inspired Taine's
preferred periods, the English and Italian Renaissance: they did
not make a distinction between the animal and the moral life, they
depicted the nude or near nude body. And, since ideas did not
impinge on pictorial representation, the head of a Greek sculpture
is not more important than its members:

When a figure displays energetic action for a given purpose, like the
"Discobulus" at Rome, the "Fighting Gladiator" in the Louvre, or the
"Dancing Faun" of Pompeii, the effect, entirely physical, exhausts
every idea and every desire within its capacity; so long as the discus is
well launched, the blow well bestowed or parried, the dance animated
and in good tune, it is satisfied, the mind making no further effort.
Generally speaking, however, the attitude is a tranquil one; the figure
does nothing, and says nothing; it is not fixed, wholly concentrated in
a profound or eager expression; it is at rest, relaxed, without weari-
ness; now standing, slightly leaning on one or the other foot, now half
turning, now half reclining.[14]

Taine's view of Greek art as harmonious, balanced and emotion-
ally undisturbed is very close to that made popular by Winckelmann.[15] The surprising thing, however, is that Taine, who in litera-

ture consistently had shown a preference for excessive emotion, should choose Winckelmann's interpretation over that of Lessing, who in his *Laokoon* (1766) attacked his learned compatriot by insisting that Greek art, far from representing calm and harmonious figures, simply tends to select one in the succession of emotional or physical states; the moment *before* pain or strain will disfigure the harmonious traits depicted.[16] Somewhat unexpected too is Taine's adoration of the nude, athletic body. True, we are told that he was a good swimmer and hiker, yet he must have spent the greatest part of his life in his study or in libraries.

What we may extract from these contradictions both with respect to his usual tastes and his daily life is that Greek art represented for him an ideal, an artistic paradise lost whose simplicity, purity and natural creations could never be recaptured by subsequent civilizations; in fact, so far from the modern mind obscured by the enormous additions of knowledge are the concepts underlying Greek art that we can scarcely still comprehend them. Being thus removed from and above modern demands, Greek sculpture satisfied Taine's intellect rather than his emotions. This quality in the critic's reactions will aid us shortly in resolving apparent inconsistencies in his *Ideal in Art*.

V *Art in the Netherlands*

A proof of the hypothesis just discussed can be found in the *Philosophy of Art in the Netherlands,* which contains a homage to Rubens. Although generally placing Flemish and Dutch painting on a lower level than Greek art, when he comes to Rubens, Taine finds no name in the history of art greater and only three or four as great as his; in fact, Rubens occupies as unique a place in Flanders as Shakespeare in England, the greatest complimentary comparison Taine can extend to any artist. Yet the reasons the critic states for his praise of Rubens reveal an artist as far removed as one can get from the Greek manner. The Flemish painter has no respect for historical or moral proprieties; on the contrary, he pushes the horrible to extremes. He is capable of depicting all of human nature save the loftiest heights. Like the Greeks, he never separates body and soul and his understanding of the latter provides the psychologist with valuable information. No wonder Taine rated him almost on a par with Shakespeare. The lines devoted to Rubens show Taine at his best in the sweeping syntheses based on careful observations which express glowing praise of a great master:

In the representation of the body, he comprehended more profoundly than any one the essential characteristic of organic life; he surpasses in this the Venetians, as they surpass the Florentines; he feels still better than they that flesh is a changeable substance in a constant state of renewal; and such, more than any other, is the Flemish body, lymphatic, sanguine and voracious, more fluid, more rapidly tending to accretion and waste than those whose dry fibre and radical temperance preserve permanent tissues. Hence it is that nobody has depicted its contrasts in stronger relief, nor as visibly shown the decay and bloom of life—at one time the dull flabby corpse, a genuine clinical mass, empty of blood and substance, livid, blue and mottled through suffering, a clot of blood on the mouth, the eye glassy and the feet and hands clayish, swollen and deformed because death seized them first; at another the freshness of living carnations, the handsome, blooming and smiling athlete, the mellow suppleness of a yielding torso in the form of a well-fed adolescent, the soft cheeks and placid candor of a girl whose blood was never quickened or eyes bedimmed by thought, flocks of dimpled cherubs and merry cupids, the delicacy, the folds. the exquisite melting rosiness of infantile skin, seemingly the petal of a flower moistened with dew and impregnated with morning light. In like manner in the representation of soul and action he appreciated more keenly than any one the essential feature of animal and moral life, that is to say the instantaneous movement which it is the aim of the plastic arts to seize on the wing. . . .

The most fleeing and most subtle shades of sentiment belong to Rubens; in this respect he is a treasure for novelist and psychologist; he took note of the passing refinements of moral expression as well as of the soft volume of sanguine flesh; no one has gone beyond him in knowledge of the living organism and of the animal man. Endowed with this sentiment and skill he was capable, in conformity with the aspirations and needs of his restored nation, of amplifying the forces he found around and within himself. all that underlie, preserve and manifest the overflow and triumph of existence.[17]

As Rubens represents Flemish *joie de vivre,* so Rembrandt illustrates the peculiarities of coloring found in Dutch painting. Contrary to Italy, the light in the Netherlands tends to go to extremes. In keeping with his temperament Rubens paints in bright colors untempered by demands for harmony or transitions. Rembrandt chose the other extreme, the moment when the light fades into obscurity, a phenomenon common in Holland.

Objects issue painfully out of shadow; they are almost lost in their surroundings; at evening, in a cellar, beneath a lamp, in an apartment into which a dying ray from a window glides, they are effaced and seem to be only more intense darks in a universal duskiness. The eye is led to noticing these gradations of obscurity, this vague train of light mingling with shadow, the remains of brightness clinging to the lingering lustre of the furniture, a reflection from a greenish window-sash, a piece of embroidery, a pearl, some golden spark astray upon a necklace. Having become sensitive to these delicacies, the painter, instead of uniting the extremes of the gamut, simply selects the beginning of it; his entire picture, except in one point, is in shadow; the concert he offers us is a continuous sordine in which now and then occurs some brilliant passage. He thus discloses unknown harmonies, those of chiaroscuro, those of modeling, those of emotion, all of them infinite and penetrating; using a daub of dirty yellow, or wine lees, or a mixed gray, or vague darks, here and there accentuated by a vivid spot, he succeeds in stirring the very depths of our nature. Herein consists the last great picturesque creation; it is through this that painting nowadays most powerfully addresses the modern mind, and this is the coloring with which the light of Holland supplied the genius of Rembrandt.[18]

Another typical aspect of Rembrandt's style can likewise be explained by the visual conditions of his country. Compared to a dry country, where the line predominates and the mountains stand out sharply against the sky, in Holland the eye is conditioned to look for other things: "Here the low horizon is without interest, and the contours of objects are softened, blended and blurred out by the imperceptible vapor with which the atmosphere is always filled; that which predominates is the spot. A cow pasturing, a roof in the centre of a field, a man leaning on a parapet appear as one tone among other tones. The object emerges; it does not start suddenly out of its surroundings as if punched out; you are struck by its modelling, that is to say by the different degrees of advancing luminousness and the diverse gradations of melting color which transforms its general tint into a relief and gives to the eye a sensation of thickness."[19]

Of the three countries Taine chose to illustrate his philosophy of art, the Netherlands prove to be the most satisfying, for, whereas the Greek portion lacks examples of art almost altogether and the Italian chapter needs to be supplemented by the travel book on Italy, in the case of the Netherlands Taine gives a masterful demonstration of his method at its best by closely joining race, milieu and moment with striking descriptions to demonstrate not only why paintings in the Netherlands are the way they are but also why those by the great artists are masterpieces.

VI   *The Ideal in Art*

Even though Taine's lectures on the *Ideal in Art* were delivered prior to those on art in the Netherlands and in Greece, in the complete volume of the lectures the author quite properly placed this section last, since it sums up by way of judgment views first theoretically exposed and then illustrated by particular examples from Italy, the Netherlands, and Greece.

One may criticize Taine on many counts, but lack of courage is definitely not among these. A scientific critic (or a naturalist, as he put it) has fulfilled his task once he has described the work of art, the conditions to which it owes its character and the state of mind it represents; in fact, we may properly question how a determinist can justify any attempt to set up a scale of values among different works of art, for are they not what they must be, given that they are the expression of prevailing conditions by means of the master faculty of the artist?

Obviously Taine had not only given serious consideration to these possible objections but he also put forth at length the arguments in favor of nondiscrimination. However, if we accept his earlier definition that the aim of a work of art is to bring out some leading and important character more effectively and clearly than attainable from real objects, then the artist forms for himself an idea of that object and transforms it according to that idea. The term "ideal" is to be taken in that sense, and consequently the work should be judged by the execution of its aim; the idea itself is of little consequence.[20] As it turns out, however, this is only one of the four following criteria Taine proposes for judging the value of works of art: *(1)* durability; *(2)* degree of importance of character; *(3)* degree of beneficence in the character; and *(4)* the converging degree of effects.

Of these the first is a traditional, historical means of measurement. Once a work has stood the test of time, chances are excellent that the diversity of opinions contained in the total judgment assures both fairness and conformity of the work to instinctive tastes. Thus highest rank can be assigned to poets such as Dante and Shakespeare, composers such as Mozart and Beethoven, and to Rubens, Rembrandt, Dürer, Titian, Leonardo da Vinci, Michelangelo and Raphael among the painters. Of course, judgment based on survival does not require a critical philosophy and may only be applied to those artists whom universal and constant acclaim has practically placed beyond discussion.

The other three yardsticks of judgment are fashioned by Taine into a grandiose scheme where each one is subdivided into an ascending hierarchy of values according to the degree of basic importance, universality of character or degree of beneficence the work in question contains. Recalling that Taine's definition of a work of art involved making predominant an essential character and reproducing accordingly the relationship of parts, the criteria based on the degree of importance of character and on the degree of convergence of effects amount to a daring but in no way unjustifiable application of the original definition to the judgment of artistic creations. For the moral evaluation derived from the beneficence in the character, however, nothing in the *Lectures on Art* had prepared the reader.

VII   *Importance of Character*

In determining the importance of character of a given work of art Taine usually measures it against five or six levels of depth corresponding either to the time span it represents or to the size of the group characterized by it. Thus, in increasing order of importance, a work may depict *(1)* fashions or fads that last from three to four years; *(2)* a movement, such as Romanticism, which covers from twenty to forty years; *(3)* an entire historical period lasting one or more centuries, such as the Middle Ages or the Renaissance; *(4)* an entire nation, e.g. the French, the English; *(5)* an entire race, e.g. Aryan, Semitic; or *(6)* all of civilized mankind.

Applied to literature, painting and sculpture, level *1* is represented by fashionable literature (the bestsellers that disappear after a few years) or by drawings or aquarelles concerned with

the dress of a particular moment such as can be found in magazines. Examples of level 2 are found in the *Astrée* of Honoré d'Urfé
or in Madeleine de Scudéry's novels (*Clélie, Le Grand Cyrus*)
which illustrate the movement of preciousness in the early seventeenth century in France. French Romanticism would be represented by Alexandre Dumas the Elder's *Antony* or Victor Hugo's
drama *Hernani*. English examples would be Lyly's *Euphues* and
Butler's *Hudibras*. In painting, this level is represented by works
limited to depicting particularities of profession, education, or the
effects of vice or virtue, passion or habit. Hogarth, Wilkie, Mulready and similar English painters fall into this literary rather than
pictorial category.

Beginning with the third level the lines are no longer so clearly
drawn. While it is true that basic national traits span a longer
time than historical periods, a work that succeeds in representing
medieval man or modern man cuts across national boundaries and
thus tends to make up in cultural breadth what it may be lacking
in national strength. Hence the gap separating levels 3 and 4 is
likely to be less great than that between levels 1 and 2. Another
problem that evidently embarrassed Taine concerns the one masterpiece by an otherwise secondary artist which displays a permanent national type, as compared with a great artist whose masterpiece or total work is limited, relatively speaking, to a historical
period. This difficulty of choice explains why *Robinson Crusoe*
and *Don Quixote* appear twice, first as examples of a period and
then as permanent national or general human types.

Seen, on level 3, as characters illustrating a historical period, we
find Gil Blas by Lesage and Manon Lescaut by the Abbé Prévost
as well as Beaumarchais' Figaro, all representatives of eighteenth-
century France; and Robinson Crusoe and Don Quixote as portrayals of their respective periods. From the Spanish picaresque
novels and the theater of Lope de Vega, Calderón and their contemporary dramatists we can realize the grandeur and misery of
the Spanish Golden Age. Racine's tragedies express the characters
and sentiments of seventeenth-century France. But the two great
epics encompassing larger historical periods in European history
are Dante's *Divine Comedy* for the Middle Ages and Goethe's
Faust for modern times. Insofar as works such as Beaumarchais'
Barber of Seville and *The Marriage of Figaro,* Racine's theater,

Robinson Crusoe and *Don Quixote* portray the Frenchman, the Englishman or the Spaniard, they may serve as examples of level *4* in literature.

In painting too, levels *3* and *4* tend to merge or else importance of character is determined by excellence of execution. It would indeed be difficult to find a valid reason for preferring, for example, the portrait of a Renaissance face to that of a typical Italian face; in fact, the latter, if there is such a thing as a permanent Italian face, is likely to be a composite and hence less appealing than the portrait of a real person. This shows that Taine's hierarchy of values originated in literature where composite characters can be frequently found. To extricate himself from this dilemma the author illustrates level *3* in painting by Italian art from Cimabue to Masaccio, when the painter, ignorant of perspective, model and anatomy, and dominated by religious sentiments, paints contours and shadows of men, sometimes glorified and incorporeal souls. To the extent to which these works represent a religious age they do thus cover a historical period.

Finally, levels *5* and *6* must also be considered together, principally because Taine cites no work dealing with an entire race. The Hebrew Psalms might best illustrate level *5,* but Taine lists them also among those masterpieces that transcend epoch, nation and race by expressing some type common to almost all of humanity. Other such grandiose creations include the *Imitation of Christ,* Homer's epics, Plato's *Dialogues,* almost all of Greek literature expressing sane and simple sentiments, Shakespeare of course, and, somewhat unexpected, once more *Don Quixote, Robinson Crusoe,* and Voltaire's *Candide.*

Again a different system must be used for painting. Since physical man is scarcely changed throughout history, execution provides the difference, rather than depth of subject matter. The painter who by his use of color records perfectly the texture of the skin, the effects of race, climate and temperament will attain the most stable elements of man, since they are inseparable from the living individual. Thus the greatest paintings are those which manifest profoundly the temperament of the artist's race. In first place are, of course, the great painters of the Italian Renaissance, followed closely by Rubens and the Spanish painters.[21]

VIII   Beneficence of Character

While the scale of values based on the importance of character
expresses Taine's philosophical view of cause by attempting to dis-
cern the most basic and general traits in man, judgment according
to the degree of beneficence of character views art from the moral
point of view. The first assigns a place to the character according
to his resistance to others, the second examines him with respect to
himself in order to see whether, left to himself, he will develop or
destroy himself or the group he belongs to. His place will therefore
depend on whether he aids or harms our life. Signs of beneficence
are the faculty to love, abnegation, disinterested acts, patriotism,
and charity. The moral order followed is, of course, not new.
Taine refers to Cicero's treatise on the *Offices* and summarizes his
basic attitude thus: "If, in two given works, both exhibit, with the
same talent in execution, natural forces of like grandeur, the one
featuring a hero is better than the one featuring a coward."[22]

At the lowest level are the weak, egotistic or common characters of realist and comical literature. Examples are those of Henri
Monnier's *Scènes de la vie bourgeoise*; Molière's Tartuffe, Orgon,
Arnolphe, and Harpagon; Sancho Panza in *Don Quixote*; the
squires, parsons, and servants in Fielding's novels; and the lower-
class figures in Balzac's *Human Comedy*. It may come as a surprise
to find Molière and Balzac, one of Taine's favorites, among authors cited, but the criticism is, of course, leveled against the character and not against the author. In fact, great artists employ two
means of concealing the mediocrity or repulsiveness of such characters: they either use them as a foil to bring out the principal
character in stronger relief (Sancho in *Don Quixote* or M. Homais
in Flaubert's *Madame Bovary*) or they turn our sympathies against
the personage who is punished for his vices (Tartuffe, or Arnolphe
in Molière's *School for Wives*). Since in physical man health, a
perfect and athletic body unencumbered by modern, tight-fitting
garments, and a balance between body and soul approach the ideal,
all manifestations of sickness or imbalance reduce the beneficence
of character in painting or sculpture. The lowest place is assigned
to the period from the fall of Rome to the Renaissance. Fatigue
and elongated necks, beginning with the epoch of Commodus and
Diocletian, flat-breasted virgins, emaciated saints, dismembered

martyrs predominate until the Renaissance restores health to art.

Next in the scale, higher than the preceding level but still negative in overall effect, are powerful but incomplete characters who are lacking in balance because of the excessive development of a passion, a faculty or disposition, in brief, monomaniacs. Consumed by pride, revenge, chivalric honor or exalted love, such personages make for excellent tragic figures in Greek, Spanish or French tragedies, in Byron and Victor Hugo, and in novels from Don Quixote down to Werther and Madame Bovary. But the great creators of monomaniacs are Shakespeare and Balzac. To say nothing of Iago, Richard III or Lady Macbeth, even the most heroic and pure among Shakespeare's characters (Hamlet, Lear, Romeo, Juliet, Desdemona, Ophelia) "are swept away either by the fury of blind imagination, the agitation of frenzied sensibility, the tyranny of flesh and blood, mental hallucination, or the irresistible flood of rage or love."[23] As for Balzac, the majority of his personages fit into this category of blind one-track minds: Baron Hulot (*Cousin Bette*), Old Goriot, Cousin Pons, Louis Lambert, and Old Grandet, to mention only a few.

The same imbalance is contained in Memling's "Hospital of Bruges" where excessively large heads, bulging foreheads and meager arms are depicted; in Fra Angelico's attenuated bodies, hollow chests and lengthened heads; in Dürer's works where thighs and arms are too thin, bellies too large, feet ungraceful and faces anxious, wrinkled and worn. Even the early Renaissance masters (Pollaiolo, Verrocchio, Luca Signorelli) still feature vulgar faces, ugly feet, painful and contorted attitudes. Nor did the Netherland artists fully embrace the new health of the Renaissance, since in Rembrandt, where primary interest is centered on light and not on man, the characters are lacking in strength, health and bodily perfections.

The positive stage is reached in level *3* by complete personages, true heroes, and perfect images of feminine innocence, goodness, virtue and delicacy. True heroes can be found in Corneille's Cid or Polyeucte; noble sentiments in Balzac's Country Doctor and Richardson's Sir Charles Grandison; feminine models in Balzac's Marguerite Claës and Eugénie Grandet or in Richardson's Pamela and Clarissa; native generosity in George Sand's Mauprat or François le Champi. Attempts to attain the highest point of the ideal have been made by superior artists, such as Goethe in *Hermann and Dorothea* and in *Iphigenia* or Tennyson in *The Idyls of the King* and in *The Princess*. In painting, the human figure achieves its full force and stature with the masters of Antwerp: Crayer, Van Oost, Van Thulden, Jordaens, but especially Rubens in whose works perfect bodies, lightly draped or nude, express health and the joy of living.

Advanced civilizations are not congenial to the creation of ideal characters. These appear rather at primitive and simple epochs, at the origins of peoples. Such perfect human types are Siegfried in the *Niebelungenlied,* Roland in the *Song of Roland,* the Cid of the Spanish Romancero, and Ulysses or Achilles in Greek literature. Not unexpectedly. the Italian Renaissance artists represent this exalted position in painting with such masterworks as Fra Bartolomeo's "St. Vincent," Raphael's "School of Athens," and Michelangelo's "Tomb of the Medicis" and the arch of the Sistine Chapel.

The highest level is reserved for revealers, saviors and gods, depicted in Homeric poems, Vedic hymns, Buddhist legends and the Scriptures. And nothing can equal these figures in art except the few remnants of Greek sculpture, such as the Venus of Milo, the Parthenon marbles or the head of Juno Queen at the Villa Ludovisi.

IX   *Convergence of Effects*

The final great yardstick for evaluating works of art is the degree of convergence of effects, or internal harmony. As the judgment of posterity, this concept is almost self-explanatory. It would be of little use to have an important and beneficent character if he were lost among a number of dispersed effects. An innate moral disposition must be linked to a physical temperament and these basic traits should be reinforced by an education, an apprenticeship, experiences and events that will fully bring out a strong and striking character. Even if this convergence may be lacking in nature, in great works of art it is always present. How many Cromwells are there in life who were born at periods that did not enable them to utilize their gifts? Imagine Mirabeau living in the seventeenth century or, conversely, Louis XVI born into a middle-class family. In art, situations and character must be in accord.

In addition to the concordance of character and inner makeup as well as exterior circumstances, a third element contributes to the convergence of effects, and that is style. Not only must the style employed be appropriate to the rest of the work, but here again art is superior to nature, for the fictional character's language is better and more consistent with his personality than that of a real human being. Whenever style and character clash, the result is inferior. Make an English character full of imagination and inner passions speak the clear and polite language of Racine, and you get the unsuccessful plays of Dryden and Otway.

While Shakespeare and Balzac illustrate the maximum convergence of effects among individual authors, the entire history of art can be judged from this point of view as well. Three stages may be observed: origins, full flowering, and decline. In the first of these talent and energy abound, but technical know-how is lacking. Such is the case in medieval French works, such as *The Song of Roland* or *Renaud de Montauban,* or in early Italian art, Giotto for example. Periods of grandeur are those in which the convergence of effects attains its perfect balance among character, action and style or, in painting, among bone and muscular structure, texture of skin, appropriate looks and physical bearing, proportions of the body and proper use of color to evoke the most suitable atmosphere. Examples of this ideal state may be found in the works of Aeschylus, Sophocles, Dante, Shakespeare, Racine, La Fontaine, Bossuet, in the tales of Voltaire and in Byron's *Don Juan*. In painting we find once more the familiar names of Leonardo da Vinci, Michelangelo, Raphael, Fra Angelico, Rembrandt and Rubens, to which are added those of Ruysdael, Poussin, Lesueur, Prud'hon, and Delacroix.

The third period in the evolution of art, decadence, is caused not by a lack of technical knowledge, which is greater than ever, but by a weakening of feelings which decline in an art dominated by routine and convention. Such are the characteristics of the theater of Euripides and of Voltaire or, in painting, they make their appearance during the second half of the sixteenth century on the canvases of the Caracci, Guido ("Saint Sebastian") or in the divergence of elements found in Flemish painters such as Bernard

Van Orley, Franz Floris, Martin de Vos and Otto Venius before
Rubens and his contemporaries reestablished the harmony of parts
in painting.

X   *The Criteria Evaluated*

Taine's four principal standards for evaluating works of art
evoke our admiration for the grandeur of his conception which
demonstrates that, in spite of unrefined instruments of humanistic
measurements, an intellectual edifice with successively superim-
posed levels can be constructed. The major criticism elicited is a
lack of harmony within the edifice itself. If this value system is to
be workable, we should expect, certainly not an automatic, but at
least a relatively consistent judgment of works across the board,
for otherwise we would fall back into the former state of anarchy
in which the vacuum of objective standards is filled by the personal taste of the critic.

A test of judgment across the board reveals that only Italian
Renaissance painting and, by implication at least, Greek sculpture
obtain consistently highest rating. In literature confusion reigns.
The Song of Roland, featuring an important and beneficent character, falls down when judged by convergence of effects; the principal characters of Shakespeare, who merit top ranking on three
counts (durability, importance, convergence), are not beneficent;
and a pale but beneficent character like Balzac's Marguerite Claës
ends up by towering above Tartuffe and Iago.

It requires no Sherlock Holmes to find the hitch in the system:
the beneficence of the character, on which most great works run
afoul. True enough, Taine had added the proviso which amounts
to "all other things being equal," but since this is never the case,
the formula is next to meaningless in practical applications. In his
desire to be logically consistent Taine omitted a permanent factor
in literature, namely that a great character should be neither entirely good nor entirely bad, a dictum that holds true not only of
modern times but dates back as far as Aristotle.

Why did Taine include moral criteria in his otherwise consistent
value system? Certainly, his previous writings had not prepared us
for this. In his *History of English Literature* the author had insisted that moral traits matter little to the scientific critic; he had even

ascribed to moral preoccupations the reason for an inherent weakness in English literature.[24] A possible hint may be found in the dedication of *The Ideal in Art* to Sainte-Beuve, his older colleague who was assuming an increasingly moral posture with time, although his life and judgment of contemporaries could hardly be cited as an example of morality or a model of Christian charity. Taine himself was no doubt a profoundly moral person and, although accepting fully the consequences of his scientific and deterministic views, he was obviously disturbed by the repeated accusation of immorality or amorality implied in his attitudes. He never tired of pointing out that one could be a determinist and yet lead a highly moral life, that, in fact, such had been the case in past examples. Our lack of information about his personal life between 1864, when the *History of English Literature* was published, and 1866, the date of the lectures on *The Ideal in Art,* does not permit any valid hypotheses.[25] What we do know, however, is the constant pressure exerted on Taine by his friends, many of whom looked with disfavor on his doctrines.

Whatever the reasons for Taine's inclusion of moral judgments in his artistic value system may be, its effect even goes counter to his personal preferences. When one considers that neither the characters of Shakespeare nor those of Stendhal and Balzac meet with moral approval, the extent of confusion this criterion creates in Taine's *Ideal in Art* becomes fully evident. There is indeed little doubt that, if the critic had been obliged to depart for that theoretical island which requires an irreparable choice of artistic companions, he would have been hard put to decide whether to take along the Venus of Milo or Rubens' "Kermesse," and he would certainly have left behind all sorts of beneficent characters in order to read for the rest of his life the stories of Hamlet, Othello, Rastignac, Fabrice del Dongo, Count Mosca and similar rascals and monomaniacs.

CHAPTER 6

The Historian

With the *Origins of Contemporary France,* which was to occupy him for the last twenty years of his life, Taine undertook his most ambitious work. If literature and art reveal the spirit and predominating attitudes of an epoch and if in this manner we understand what the English and French race or character are like, this is indeed precious knowledge for penetrating into the intellectual and psychological causes that made individuals or groups feel and think the way they did. To crown Taine's life work only one more addition was needed: seeing these human beings in action, and only a philosophical historian capable of drawing on psychology, literature and art could describe and explain an entire age in all its living complexity.

I *Taine's Concept of Explicative History*

By now it is hardly necessary to repeat what has already been said about Taine's literary and artistic criticism: that he did not intend to write an ordinary history of modern France any more than he had planned to deal descriptively with the history of English literature. Already in his *Essay on Livy* Taine had belittled the conscientious chroniclers who spare the reader no detail; instead he had favored an explicative history written by a philosophical historian:

Another means of bringing out laws is to choose among the facts. How the narration drags on when all of them are told! What is the use, after recounting in a war twenty combats and pillagings, to go on with the monotonous recital of skirmishes that are always the same? To tell everything is to tell too much; one must not tire the mind nor clutter up science. . . . The historian heads straight for the general idea through the facts which prove it, stops only in order to explain better by means of impressive details and to show the end of his trip on the horizon. One feels with him that one is going somewhere and progressing; the narration becomes interesting because the facts are chosen. . . .

To group the facts under laws which complete and prove them, to tie particular laws to universal ones, either by arranging the narration or by choosing among the details or by summing up the theories through imaginative insights, these are the characteristics of a historian.[1]

As in his preceding works Taine declares that "every event, whatever it may be, is conditioned, and, its conditions being given, when these conditions are present, it never fails to occur. . . . Human history is a thing of natural growth like the rest; its direction is due to its own elements; no external force guides it, but the inward forces that create it; it is not tending to any prescribed end but developing a result."[2] It is a credit to Taine as a consistent thinker and to the basic validity of his method that the same working basis can be applied to the study of a literary, an artistic or a historical problem. For here again it is a question of determining which were the generative factors, those great active and permanent forces that carry in their wake an enormous mass of other functions. To these must be added more or less accidental and disturbing elements in order to determine the final result.[3] Thus the author was once again applying the tripartite theory of race, milieu and moment, this time not to a study of a foreign nation but to his own. The race is the French character, conditioned by a long Classical tradition and inflected through the new ideas of the eighteenth-century philosophers and Rousseau's *Social Contract*; the milieu is above all social and political: that of an unhappy and discontented lower class, burdened by hunger and taxes, of a rising middle class that sees its ambitions thwarted, and of a nobility and a clergy discredited by the abuses of their privileges; the moment is that of a breakdown of authority due to the cumulative weakening of the king and the nobles, a decadence caused both by the loss of virility that drawing-room life entails and by the new belief in the goodness of human nature.

II *Taine's Attitude and Purpose*

A number of reasons made Taine abandon literature and art for the history of modern France. In 1849 he had already refused to commit himself politically because he felt that to do so would require a knowledge of what the French people are like and what is best for them. In 1854, while forced to take a rest, he had the *History of the French Revolution* by Buchez and Roux read to him; surprised by the intellectual mediocrity of the most famous revolutionaries, he thought that this would be an interesting historical problem to investigate. About 1863, in his chapter on Carlyle, he still chides the English writer for the very attitude of criticizing the French Revolution which he was to adopt later on himself: "But set the good beside the evil; put down virtues beside vices! These sceptics believed in demonstrated truth, and would have her alone for mistress. These logicians founded society only on justice, and risked their lives rather than renounce an established theorem. These epicureans embraced in their sympathies entire humanity. . . . They fought against evil in society, as the Puritans fought it in the soul. They were generous, as the Puritans were virtuous. They had, like them, a heroism, but sympathetic, sociable, ready to proselytise, which reformed Europe, whilst the English one only served England."[4]

At that time Taine still shared the view held by the majority of the French that the Revolution, despite the excesses of the Terror, had generally been beneficial; however, in the account of his trip to Italy in 1864, critical references to the Revolution begin to appear. A firsthand observation of a popular uprising, the Paris Commune from March 18 to May 28, 1870, which resulted in 20,000 casualties, deeply impressed the historian and a growing pessimism about the future of France's Third Republic induced him to examine the suffering body politic. Thus despite his assurances that, as a natural scientist studying the metamorphosis of an insect, he would describe the changeover in France from *Ancien Régime* to Revolution to New Régime, a new note appears in the explicative tone of the supposedly detached scientist: he sees his work as a medical consultation, and the patient is France whose political structure, fixed permanently by 1808, has made the country suffer from an illness comparable to an attack of syphilis.[5] This "medical" approach implies not only a judgment, namely that modern France is sick, but it also obliges the physician to prescribe a cure for the ailing patient.

Since Taine's death prevented him from carrying his work through to the late nineteenth century, the *Origins of Contemporary France* is centered around the Revolution with the *Ancien Régime* forming the prologue and the New Régime the epilogue. In the eleven-volume edition these three periods take up two, six, and three volumes, respectively. Aside from a study of the changes in the political and social structure of modern France, Taine's work offers four principal features: *(1)* the presentation of the basic causes that led to the Revolution; *(2)* a study of Jacobin, of mass and mob psychology; *(3)* a severe criticism of the Revolution; and *(4)* the author's diagnosis of France's illness and his suggestions of what should have been done to prevent it. In this way Taine was embarking on another pioneer work whose application of causal theory forecast the future efforts of Arnold Toynbee. No one before him in France had consulted original documents, that were gathering dust in the National Archives, with such thoroughness in order to bolster his theses with an impressive array of statistics which, in spite of some inaccuracies, opened new avenues to modern historians.

III   *The Causes of the Revolution*

Taine speaks primarily of two causes that were responsible for the revolutionary spirit, but all through the two volumes dealing with the *Ancien Régime* six causes can be found that led to the French Revolution. Three of these are material, while the other three (and in this Taine's original approach to history is illustrated) are due to intellectual currents or certain states of mind. The material factors had been previously noted by Alexis de Tocqueville in the *Ancien Régime and the Revolution* (1856). They were the abuse of privileges by the nobles and the clergy who were no longer rendering equivalent services to the nation and hence had become a financial burden. Similarly, the royal government had been treating the state as if it were its personal property and was guilty of arbitrary waste. Consequently, to pay for this fiscal irresponsibility, the commoners had been taxed so heavily that the workers, and the peasants especially, were reduced to a state of permanent poverty with famine threatening to break out at any time, a situation which fomented a discontent needing only a breakdown in authority to turn into revolt. But this social cancer, even though more malignant by 1789, had plagued France for close to a century. Why did it prove to be fatal for the *Ancien Régime* at that particular time? A corrosion of authority had taken place concurrently, not caused by external pressure but by both a physical weakening process in the nobility and a change in the intellectual view of nature, society and man. One has only to compare Louis XIV with his two successors in order to realize the decline in energy, will power, and administrative talent which had sapped the strength of royal authority.

All this was not new at the time Taine wrote the *Ancien Régime*. His original approach consists in the special attention he pays to the distillation of the intellectual atmosphere which, on the one hand, contributed to the near collaboration of the nobility in its own destruction and, on the other hand, encouraged the commoners to revolt against the royal government. Two primary ingredients, salutary when separate but poisonous as a mixture, went into the making of eighteenth century philosophy. The first of these, we have already encountered:[6] the Classical spirit of the seventeenth and eighteenth centuries with its reigning model of the "honnête homme," its drawing-room society, its characteristics of orderly and logical presentation, step-by-step progression by means of carefully arranged transitions, and constant development. In his essay on Racine, Taine had called this spirit "oratorical reasoning"; here the term used is "reasoning reason" (*la raison raisonnante*), "requiring the least preparation for thought, giving itself as little trouble as possible, content with its acquisitions, taking no pains to increase or renew them, incapable of, or unwilling to embrace the plenitude and complexity of actualities."[7] These characteristics, which can produce great works when kept within bounds, grow even stronger in the eighteenth century until the *raison raisonnante* ends up expressing only commonplaces, elegantly to be sure, but for practical purposes "of little, none, or dangerous service."[8]

Concomitant weaknesses of the Classical spirit include an insufficient sense of history, the habit of neglecting what is particular and a conception of human beings as simple generalized automatons whose mechanism is known. Thus French novels of the eighteenth century rarely mention profession, wealth or even marital status of the characters, and in plays almost no distinction is made

among Turks, Arabs, Greeks, or Romans. The same defect is
found in most historians except occasionally in Voltaire. "To pur-
sue in every research, with the most confidence, without either
reserve or precaution, the mathematical method; to derive, limit
and isolate a few of the simplest generalized notions; and then,
setting experience aside, comparing them, combining them, and,
from the artificial compound thus obtained, deducing all the consequences they involve by pure reasoning, is the natural process
of the Classical spirit."[9]

The second ingredient is scientific progress. Newton is, of course,
the greatest innovator with calculus and his contributions in astronomy and physics. With the movements of the planets and their
satellites explained and predictable, the decomposition of light
and the velocity of sound formulated, the foundations of chemistry
provided by the work of Scheele, Priestley, Cavendish, Stahl and
the theory of Lavoisier, the entire history of our globe proposed
by Buffon, botanic nomenclature and classifications contributed
by Linnaeus, and the leading features of modern physiology and
zoology outlined by Buffon and Lamarck, a new concept of man
and the world emerges which reduces man to an atom in nature
and, instead of considering him as an empire within an empire,
sees him now as a part of the whole creation. The eighteenth century philosophers, contrary to their predecessors, all practice science and apply the scientific method based on observable facts to
human affairs, a procedure of which Taine wholeheartedly approves.
There exist, however, two dangers: the method is only as good as
the competence of those who use it, and the philosophers meet the
requirement but halfway; besides, they are still imbued with the
Classical spirit, which will incline them to proceed in an a priori
fashion.

Into this dangerous and, according to Taine, poisonous mixture
of Classical spirit and scientific progress, which establishes reason
as the new God, falls a drop of philosophy that will serve as a
catalyst: Rousseau's cry of the return to nature, expressed both in
his conception of man as good and reasonable but corrupted by
society and in the *Social Contract* which is at the same time an-
archistic and despotic. These new ideas penetrate into the drawing
rooms where they are discussed and eventually accepted. So strong
is the belief in the goodness of the people, that the majority of the

nobles will take no drastic measures against the revolutionaries, so that their gentleness of spirit and manner will eventually turn them into sheep reduced to be slaughtered in a heroic stance.

With the *Ancien Régime* ready to fall like an overripe plum, the new ideas merely have to move from the drawing rooms into the street, where they will enter the ill-educated minds of the future revolutionary leaders, in order for the social and political explosion to burst out.

IV   *Jacobin, Mass, and Mob Psychology*

Two theses run through Taine's volumes on the French Revolution. The first refutes the general view that the Revolution had begun as a benign reform movement which suddenly turned into violence and finally into the Terror because its best elements became dominated by the most subversive ones. Taine insists that, right from the beginning, it aimed at the complete destruction of the old order. The impulses of this movement led the masses toward a spontaneous anarchy, from there to legal anarchy and quite inevitably to the Reign of Terror because control had been taken over by the most extreme factions. As the extremist leaders devoured each other, the level of leadership kept sinking lower until it came into the hands of the most violent and bloodthirstry demagogues. Once these had disappeared, with the end of the Terror, Napoleon emerged, reorganized the State and founded the institutions of modern France. Taine's other thesis maintains that, in spite of the appealing slogans of liberty, equality, fraternity, the Revolution was essentially a transfer of property, and that we must look to this master passion for its chief support, its enduring energy, its primary impulse and its historical significance.[10]

A revolution provides an excellent study of psychology and Taine delves deeply into the minds of the masses, the mobs, and the leaders. His findings, if accepted, would suffice to discourage the most fervent advocates of radical social change. Revolution, Taine claims, is dominated by those who shout loudest and brings to the surface the dregs of society. Whereas the law-abiding, hardworking citizens, too busy with their daily tasks, frightened by the violent atmosphere, and rendered passive by the centralization of the *Ancien Régime,* lacked initiative, the radical group at the Palais-Royal, the future Jacobin supporters, consisted of idlers, malcontents, café philosophers, vagabonds, perverts, and similar trash, a minority that claimed to represent the people and imposed its will on the Constituent and Legislative Assemblies and on the Convention. This dictatorship of a mob, during conditions of anarchy, forced the leaders not to lead from above but take orders from below and to follow the blind impulses of their supporters. Under these circumstances the beast, always lurking beneath the veneer of civilization in man, is released and carries out its wanton destruction. By the end of 1792 France is ruled over from Paris by "five thousand brutes and blackguards with two thousand hussies" and the country "resembles a human being forced to walk on his head and to think with his feet."[11]

Why did this first application of the social sciences to human affairs turn out to be such a disaster? Taine finds part of the answer in the low intellectual caliber of the revolutionary leaders. The majority was composed of second-rate lawyers whose experience of life was limited to legal chicaneries and paper work, but the Jacobins also included unknown writers, journalists, and students scarcely out of school, in short, half-educated people who lived by slogans and were incapable of carrying out the delicate social experiment which required empirical statesmanship. Brought up in the Classical tradition these new leaders thought only in simple terms of good and bad: man in general, the rights of man, the social contract, liberty, equality, reason, nature, the people, the tyrants—these notions, mere words, took in their minds the place of real human beings and of real situations. By the time the Terror began, the revolutionary idiot had developed in whom only two fixed ideas remained: murder and the public safety. This mental rigidity led to the destruction of monuments and of the productive capacities of towns that were to be punished for insurrection. Taine compares these Jacobin actions to the furor of the Mongols of the fifth and thirteenth centuries:

One can understand how the Mongols, who were nomads, desired to convert the soil into one vast steppe. But, to demolish a town whose arsenal and harbor is maintained by it, to destroy the leaders of manufacturing interests and their dwellings in a city where its workmen and factories are preserved, to keep up a fountain and stop the stream which flows from it, or the stream without the fountain is so absurd that the idea could only enter the head of a Jacobin. His contracted mind is so worked up that he is no longer aware of contradictions; the ferocious stupidity of the barbarian and the fixed idea of the inquisitor meet on common ground; the earth is not big enough for any but himself and the orthodox of his species. Employing absurd, inflated and sinister terms he decrees the extermination of heretics: not only shall their monuments, dwellings and persons be destroyed, but every vestige of them shall be eradicated and their names lost to the memory of man.[12]

One may explain these excesses perpetrated by minor revolutionaries, such as Fréron and Carrier, by the enormous difference between what they were before the Revolution and the sultanic power suddenly thrust upon them, but how are we to understand the great revolutionary leaders: Marat, Danton, Robespierre, and Saint-Just? The historian devotes a long analysis to each of these men and for each he tries to determine the master faculty. If Taine's psychological case study of these men is even half correct, then one is forced to conclude that rarely in the history of modern times has a political movement been led by a similar quartet of maniacs.

Marat receives the most uncomplimentary treatment, since he rates at best as instigator and barker, not as a leader. His master faculty is the same as that of the Revolution: suspicious delirium and homicidal monomania. Taine cannot find terms harsh enough for Marat calling him, upon the occasion when he received full powers from the Convention, on June 2, 1793, a foul abortion, a charlatan, monomaniac and murderer.[13] By contrast, the most sympathetic portrayal is reserved for Danton whom Taine considers a true leader of men, the only one among the revolutionaries capable of coordinated action in the general chaos. Possessing political gifts, he had, under a butcher's temperament, the heart of a man and thus saved political adversaries contrary to the desires of Marat and Robespierre. Still "in temperament he is a *barbarian* . . . born to command his fellow creatures like this or that vassal of the sixth century or baron of the tenth century . . . With a thundering voice . . . full-blooded, boiling over with passion and energy, . . . roaring like a bull when speaking, . . . able to arouse savage instincts in the most tranquil breast and generous instincts in the most brutal, . . . full of crude jests worthy of Rabelais, possessing a stock of jovial sensuality and good humor, cordial and familiar in his ways, frank, friendly in tone; in short, outwardly and inwardly the best fitted for winning the confidence and sympathy of a Gallic, Parisian populace."[14]

While Marat and Danton are opposites, Robespierre and Saint-Just complement each other. If Marat deserved contempt, Robespierre is singled out as the greatest viper of the Revolution. A lunatic who is logical, a monster that pretends to have a conscience, a hypocrite believing himself sincere, a Cain who regarded himself as an Abel, a theologian who would become an inquisitor, a *cuistre*.[15] Taine is having a field day piling enough master faculties on Robespierre to make him burst. But the author of *On Intelligence* never forgets to deduce the psychological consequences of basic dispositions:

> Robespierre, from the beginning to the end of the Revolution, is always, in his own eyes, Robespierre the unique, the one pure man, the infallible and the impeccable; no man ever burnt to himself the incense of his own praise so constantly and so directly. . . .
>
> Thus is this character rounded off like that of the theologian who would become an inquisitor. Extraordinary contrasts meet in its formation—a lunatic that is logical, and a monster that pretends to have a conscience. Under the pressure of his faith and egotism, he had developed two deformities, one of the head and the other of the heart; his common sense is gone, and his moral sense is utterly perverted. In fixing his mind on abstract formulas, he is no longer able to see men as they are; through self-admiration he finally comes to viewing his adversaries, and even his rivals, as miscreants deserving of death. On this down-hill road nothing stops him, for, in qualifying things inversely to their true meaning, he has violated within himself the precious conceptions which bring us back to truth and justice. No light reaches eyes which regard blindness as clear-sightedness; no remorse affects a soul which erects barbarism into patriotism, and which sanctions murder with duty.[16]

Next to these three "truly remarkable animals" (the expression is Taine's in the Preface to Volume III), Saint-Just pales, being Robespierre's pupil as the latter is Rousseau's. A man who began by stealing from his mother, a calcified student haunted by bloody memories of Rome and Sparta, a warped intelligence that finds itself at ease in the realm of the enormous paradox and the shameless sophism, Saint-Just ranks no higher in that peculiar kingdom of moral zoology than "a sententious and over-excited declaimer, an artifical spirit always on the stretch, full of affectations, . . . confining himself to theatrical and funereal paradoxes, a sort of 'grand vizier' with the airs of an exalted moralist and the bearing of the sentimental shepherd."[17]

True to his contention that each talent needs a propitious milieu in order to flourish, Taine speculates that, without the Revolution, Marat would probably have ended up in an insane asylum, Danton hanged after a career as a filibuster or a bravo, while Robespierre would have assumed the place of a hard-working lawyer in good standing with moderate success as author of moral essays and winner of competitive prizes awarded by provincial academies.

V Criticism of the Revolution

From an ideology containing the Classical spirit and Rousseau's *Social Contract* and a movement led by men who vary intellectually from mediocre to idiotic and insane not much can be expected. Taine's indictment of the French Revolution is unrelenting, both for its philosophical assumptions and its actions. In view of the general approval the Revolution enjoyed during his time and with French politics taking a turn to the left in 1875, he saw his task as one of unmasking a movement whose glittering exterior was hiding a serpent underneath. That is why he chose to open his description of the revolutionary government with a parable: " 'In Egypt,' says Clement of Alexandria, 'the sanctuaries of the temples are shaded by curtains of golden tissue. But on going further into the interior in quest of the statue, a priest of grave aspect, advancing to meet you and chanting a hymn in the Egyptian tongue, slightly raises a veil to show you the god. And what do you behold? A crocodile, or some indigenous serpent, or other dangerous animal, the Egyptian god being a brute rolling about on a purple carpet.' "[18]

In trying to explain what went wrong with the Revolution, Taine criticizes its basic assumptions and singles out the Classical spirit and Rousseau's political theories, in particular the *Social Contract,* for special blame. Having been raised in a system of abstractions which had a preconceived notion of man in general without taking into consideration the peculiar needs of real human beings formed by the influence of race, milieu and moment, i.e., people living in a definite historical situation, the revolutionary thinkers were predisposed to accept the theories of the *Social Contract* which is not a historical pact, since it recognizes no anterior rights. The same abstract state of mind likewise led to the drawing up of a constitution not for the French people of the late eighteenth century but for theoretical beings who might as well live on the moon.

The clash between Rousseau and Taine was, of course, inevitable. The man who always perceived the mad ape underneath man's polished veneer and who believed in the inviolable right to own property could not possibly admit that man is good and generous by nature and that property amounts to theft. In addition Taine exposed the basic inconsistencies in the *Social Contract* and their harmful effects when applied to a real social situation. On the one hand, by making the existing form of government subject to the will of the people at any given moment, the *Social Contract* leads to a permanent state of anarchy; on the other hand, by alienating all individual rights and property to the community, Rousseau's theory leads to despotism. The resulting society resembles a secular convent in which all possessions, the education of children, and the decision as to which religion is to be practiced are handed over to the state.

In its despotism the new contract continues the type of government that existed under the *Ancien Régime* with this difference, that the new sovereign is no longer the king but the people. "This constitutes the final result and complete triumph of the classic spirit. Installed in narrow brains, incapable of entertaining two related ideas, it is to become a cold or furious monomania, maddened in the destruction of a past it curses, and in the establishment of the millennium it pursues, and all in the name of an imaginary contract, at once anarchical and despotic, which unfetters insurrection and justifies dictation; all to end in a social antagonism, resembling now a bacchanalian orgy of demons, and now a Spartan conventual group; all with a view to substitute for the existing man, enduring and slowly formed by history, an improvised automaton that is to fall away through its own debility when the external and mechanical force that keeps it up will no longer sustain it."[19]

The consequences of the fall of the *Ancien Régime* and the application of the *Social Contract* by inexperienced men of mediocre caliber impoverished by Classical principles can be readily foreseen. The spontaneous anarchy caused by the overthrow of a regime that had lasted for nearly two hundred years was reinforced by the anarchical elements of the *Social Contract* which rendered orderly government impossible, since its insistence that the people's will be respected at all times reduced the elected representatives to lackeys who had to bow before the constantly changing demands of their constituents. The sessions of both the Constituent and Legislative Assemblies resembled a circus dominated by the galleries which were packed, moreover, by paid agitators of the radical Jacobins. In their impractical idealism even the more respectable representatives practically committed suicide by agreeing that members of the Constituent Assembly would not be eligible to serve in the Legislative Assembly; in the same manner they closed to themselves the possibility of participating in the executive branch of the government as ministers. As a consequence and by means of intimidating tactics the most radical, although a minority, took over control and before the Constituent Assembly was dissolved, more than four hundred of its members were in flight or reduced to silence.

When the Jacobins come to power they do not restore orderly government but merely turn the spontaneous anarchy into a legitimate one designed to serve their purposes. Throughout Taine's six volumes on the French Revolution a succession of plunderings by unlawful bands of brigands, of nobles or people in authority being threatened, attacked, harmed or killed, of heads being carried on sticks by strutting beings half man half monkey, of brutal passions being unleashed, of entire towns given over to the savage instincts of brutes like Carrier and Fréron ruling with the unlimited power of an Oriental sultan over Nantes and Toulon respectively, of towns suffering destruction as punishment for insurrection, of heads rolling mechanically off the guillotine in the cold, self-righteous blood bath of the Terror pass before the reader's horrified eyes. Even those most sympathetic to the aims of the French Revolution will be unable to suppress an involuntary shudder at imagining so many atrocities and, even if only half of these were proven beyond dispute, they would suffice to tarnish forever the image of an idealistic movement that got occasionally out of hand, an impression not infrequently conveyed in the accounts of French historians prior to Taine.[20]

In a marginal note the author surveyed the wreckage left behind by the "Neros of the gutter" and Napoleon, their brilliant but egotistical successor: "The important thing is not to go into bankruptcy to the tune of forty billion [francs], or to have twenty-two million people killed, to be invaded, stripped of resources. . . . The French Revolution was an immense assault on the persons and property of citizens, the Empire against the persons and property of foreigners. . . . Summary of the Revolution: France, as Esau, ceded its birthright in Europe for a dish of lentils."[21]

VI *What Should Have Been Done*

Up to this point, despite a pitch of indignation not previously encountered in his works, Taine has followed his general method: discovering the causes of a phenomenon in order to explain its effects. Being human, the historian may give vent to his reactions of sadness or disgust when ordinary people are driven or permitted to unchain the animal in them that causes them to commit atrocities. Moral preoccupations, it will be remembered, had entered Taine's work already with the beneficence of character category in *The Ideal in Art*. So far a scientific historian who believes in determinism may go, but no further. Having convincingly illustrated why the *Ancien Régime* had to fall and having explained the psychological and intellectual makeup of the revolutionary leaders and crowds, all there was left was to watch the sad spectacle unfold itself. The patriot might regret that France at that time was not granted an unusual leader, wise beyond the limits of time and circumstances, who miraculously would have managed the peaceful transition from monarchy to popular government, but Taine was an unvarying opponent of miracles.

Judging from his great admiration for the Italian Renaissance, we might have expected him to draw an exciting portrait of his own people who, for once in their history, were acting the way the Italians had three centuries earlier. But Taine, who took pleasure in writing about these beautiful beasts of the past, did not display the same attitude when it came to his compatriots of the Revolution. A tiger in a cage or in foreign lands centuries ago is far more attractive than one the effects of whose actions can still be felt. Besides, Renaissance manners do not suit the French character and the spectacle produced was far less colorful and elegant than the Florentine pageants Taine describes in his *Lectures on Art*. Moreover, the eventual rigor mortis of the mind of a Robespierre during the Terror renders the total effect produced far from pleasing.

At any rate, Taine, instead of depicting these revolutionary beasts and monsters in the manner of a zoologist, metes out blame; instead of accepting the inevitable consequences which follow once a set of circumstances are present, he veers from the path of determinism and proposes what should have been done. This new attitude differed from his criticism of Racine and the spirit of the seventeenth century, which he found wanting in many ways but the consequences of which he accepted. By insisting that the leaders should have unhooked one of the links in the fateful chain of events and mended it in such a way as to avoid a radical change in the direction French political and social life would take, the philosophical historian takes a number of dangerous risks: *(1)* he may be judging with the wisdom which is attributable to hindsight; *(2)* he may be asking of a group of human beings what they were incapable of in view of their capacities, their experience, and the emotional atmosphere in which they found themselves; *(3)* he may be criticizing by means of measuring the actions committed during a period in the past against his own political beliefs held a century later.

One is indeed struck by the disparity between the force of Taine's criticism of both the *Ancien Régime* and of the Revolution and the weakness of the solutions proposed.[22] He does make an eloquent plea for the importance of tradition, that "hereditary prejudice" based on a long accumulation of experience, for traditions which cannot prove their rights by logical demonstration, for the important role that the state, the nobility and the clergy had occupied for a millennium in France. He is correct in pointing out that an ignorance of history and the erection of unempirical reason as supreme ruler contemptuous of tradition was likely to result in an unwise course of action. We can even agree that a sage legislator would have first studied what the French were like in 1789 in order to devise for them the kind of constitution best suited for them and that a nation in which 20,000,000 citizens had not advanced far beyond the mental state of the Middle Ages (an exaggeration, per-

haps, but valid even when the figure is cut in half) was not ready
to assume the functions of a pure democracy.

Perhaps, if a revolution had occurred in 1875, these factors
might have been taken into consideration, but it would have been
too much to expect of the revolutionary leaders who suddenly
found enormous responsibilities thrust upon them and who had
in no way been prepared for leadership by a century and a half
of centralized, monarchical government. Taine also ignores or pays
little attention to the emotional atmosphere created by the rumors
of conspiracies, the fear that the Revolution would be betrayed
and the Bourbons returned to power. Moreover, he passes lightly
over the exterior threats to the Revolution. "The Emigrés on the
Rhine, the ceaseless intrigues of the Court with foreign powers, the
flight [of Louis XVI] to Varennes, the hostile armies massed on
the frontier a few days' march from the capital, the savage threats
of the Brunswick manifesto, the rebellion in the West—these menacing facts, without which the domestic history is unintelligible, are
left virtually unnoticed."[23]

"During the night of July 14-15, 1789, the Duc de la
Rochefoucauld-Liancourt caused Louis XVI to be aroused to
inform him of the taking of the Bastille. 'It is a revolt, then?'
exclaimed the King. 'Sire!' replied the Duke, 'it is a revolution!' "
Thus begins Taine's study of the French Revolution and, as we
have seen, his thesis is that it was neither a revolt nor a revolution, but a dissolution. Yet the remedies he proposes seem hardly
adequate to deal with a palace uprising. He claims that the reforms proposed by the King in his declaration of June 25, 1789,
decreeing that the budget would have to be henceforth approved
by the States-General and providing for a more equitable distri-
bution of the tax burden would have sufficed to remedy the basic
ills of the *Ancien Régime*. But it was obviously too late for such
moderate reforms and the people could hardly be expected to trust
the promises of the royal government on its past record. Equally
unrealistic is Taine's assertion that leadership should have been
entrusted to the liberal aristocracy and that "some considerations
for them, some outward signs of respect, a few bows, would, in
all probability, have rallied them sincerely to democratic institutions."[24] Aside from its debatable assumption, this attitude betrays
a surprising lack of psychological insight into what must have been

the feelings of the French people whose egalitarian principles had for generations led them to resent those very outward signs of respect and the bows connected with them. To ask these people to place their revolution into the hands of a thoroughly discredited social class amounts to confusing an increasingly enraged population with a group of well-behaved school children.

More reasonable is Taine's observation that qualified leaders could have been found among those who had had previous experience in some government functions: the *intendants* and the military commanders of every province, prelates who administered large dioceses, local judges, and respected members of provincial assemblies.[25] But those who had occupied official positions under the *Ancien Régime* were necessarily engulfed in the maelstrom of criticism which the abuses of that government had aroused and they were looked upon somewhat the way collaborators were after the liberation of France in World War II. Besides, the very inability of these former officials and of the nobility to undertake decisive action in their own self-defense, even if imputable to the best of motives, demonstrates their obvious malaise and their lack of vitality at a time when only the strongest could survive.

While Taine's proposed remedies prove to be quite inadequate for curing the ills to be treated, they reveal the author's own political convictions and must be viewed partly as being addressed to the contemporary state of political affairs. Taine's stand can best be defined as a preference for a liberal aristocracy. At the basis of his political philosophy lies his concern for the inviolability of the individual and of property. Consequently he is unalterably opposed to the centralized state and to despotism, whether exerted by an individual or by the mob. His accusation against the *Ancien Régime* as well as the revolutionary government is that both centralized political power (in Versailles and Paris, respectively) and effectively dictated what the people were to think, how they were to arrange their lives, how their children were to be educated, what associations were permitted, thus depriving the individual of liberty and initiative, destroying the possibility of free and private associations, and condemning the French provinces to intellectual and economic stagnation. Convinced that the French were not ripe for democratic government, he looked for a model to England where a vigorous aristocracy was actively engaged in governing the country. While aware that governments cannot be transplanted, he chided the *Ancien Régime* for having reduced the nobles to a useless class so that the resulting vacuum was filled by the untrained, incapable middle and lower classes, a development that led to the rise of the professional politicians, such as govern the United States of America.[26]

Rarely have the power-grabbing impulses of the centralized state been more virulently attacked than by Taine. Somewhat unexpectedly, his distrust of human nature did not lead him to the Hobbesian defense of the despot. Instead he stipulated that the power of the state should be limited to those functions that a voluntary association of private or local citizens cannot assume: police, army, courts, national roads, and sanitation. This attitude explains why Taine, anticlerical and critical of the Church during the *Ancien Régime,* rallies to defend religion when it is persecuted during the Revolution. Although he eventually came to look upon the Church as a "moral gendarme," this view does not justify the claim that Taine had returned to Catholicism. He accepted only the social value of religion.[27]

VII   *Napoleon and Modern France*

Whatever issue one may take with Taine's views, his courage and integrity deserve our admiration, for he dared attack two of France's most sacred cows: the Revolution and Napoleon. Taine saw in Napoleon not a traitor to the Revolution, but its natural end result. The Revolution had adopted the anarchical elements of Rousseau's *Social Contract*; Napoleon will apply the despotic principles of Rousseau's political treatise. Across the Revolution Napoleon established a bridge between the New and the *Ancien Régime,* for in the "philosophical barracks" he built for the French, in his centralized, efficiently administered state, fabricated logically on a general and simple principle, he achieved what had merely been a dream for Richelieu, Louis XIV and Mirabeau, and what the previous regimes had prepared for him.

The continuity Taine establishes between the three governments he studied brings out his most intimate accusation against the Revolution. He views it not only as a period of popular debauchery, as "the revolt of the donkeys and horses against man,"[28] as a transfer of wealth, as a period of savage murders committed by rigid doctrinaires, but, above all, as a unique and missed opportunity to divert France from its apparently predestined form of government which regiments individual freedom and shackles its institutions in a strait jacket of administrative uniformity. As he looked at conditions prevailing in France in his own times, Taine saw only a future of eternal vacillation between the anarchy of socialist or popular government and the rule by a despot, monarchical or otherwise.

Napoleon was fateful for France in more than one way, for by 1808 he had cast the mold into which French institutions would henceforth have to fit. Taine presents a portrait of Napoleon that is far from unsympathetic. Prior to the publication of his article on the Emperor in the *Revue des Deux Mondes* Taine had told the Princess Matilde how he judged her uncle: "the greatest genius of the modern world and an egoism equal to his genius." The two faculties (genius and egoism) dominate in the historian's treatment of Napoleon. His master faculty was the constructive imagination of an artist locked up in politics but his master passion was prideful self-love. As a statesman he possessed all the gifts the Jacobins were lacking: superior intelligence, practical intuition, an empirical way of acting, a profound knowledge of human nature and of the French in particular. As a person Napoleon was a complete egoist, incapable of love, unsociable, creating an atmosphere of uneasiness around him, but at the same time given to angry outbursts that betrayed the Corsican in him. Taine is obviously fascinated neither by the man nor by his legend and more interested in his role as the builder of modern France than in his personal life.

VIII *Conclusions*

The weaknesses of Taine's *Origins of Contemporary France* are apparent and he has generally been severely criticized by subsequent historians. Both Paul Lacombe and A. Aulard[29] take him to task for his anti-popular prejudices, his weak solutions, and for faulty or incomplete references. Serious as these accusations may be, they are less grave than that concerning Taine's use of witnesses. The overwhelming majority of his quotations come from foreign observers who were hostile to, or suspicious of, the Revolution. Foremost among these is Mallet du Pan, a Swiss citizen and royalist who sent reports on French affairs to the Austrian Emperor and to the cabinets of Turin and Lisbon. He left France in 1792; yet Taine considered him the most competent, the most judicious and profound observer of the Revolution. Just behind Mallet du Pan, rank Arthur Young, an Englishman living in France during the Revolution; Governor Morris, the American ambassador to France; and an English lady writing about her experiences during the Terror under the name of Anne Plumptree but whose real identity is suspected to have been John Gifford, an extreme anti-Jacobin. Among Frenchmen only Malouet, a royalist, and Mirabeau are quoted at any length.

Along with Taine's chapter on Shakespeare in the *History of English Literature,* the *Origins of Contemporary France* is his most impassioned work. In the former he boiled over with enthusiasm, in the latter with indignation. Such excessive emotions are of course impediments for a philosophical and explicative work. We should note in passing that Taine succeeded better in constructive criticism, as witnessed by his treatment of Shakespeare and Stendhal, than in destructive writings, such as his attacks on Racine and the French Revolution. But he did achieve part of his goal in demonstrating how a historian can write philosophically by searching for the causes of events in the intellectual and psychological states of mind that lead to them, and how his method, already applied to literature and art, could be fertile in the writing of history. The method employed by Arnold J. Toynbee in his celebrated *A Study of History* (London, 1935-1961) is not far removed from Taine's.

The Origins of Contemporary France stirred up enormous interest and passionate debate in France. Thirty-one printings of the work have appeared to date which, considering that it comprises eleven volumes, places it among the bestselling historical studies of its kind. The reason for its success is that, despite considerable shortcomings, it remains eminently readable and that it counteracts the predominantly favorable attitude of historians of the French Revolution. "Of books that are strong enough to work a change and form an epoch in a reader's life," declared Acton, "there are two perhaps on our revolutionary shelf. One is Taine, and the other Michelet. No man feels the grandeur of the Revolution till he reads Michelet, or the horror of it without reading Taine."[30]

CHAPTER 7

Taine's Achievements and Influence

"Flaubert remarked of the *History of English Literature* that it got rid of the uncritical notion that books dropped like meteorites from the sky."[1] Taine accomplished far more than that. His was an ambitious inquiry, not about abstract man, but about men, different groups of men living in different countries and conditions at different times. Unless we keep in mind that his ultimate goal was an understanding of men rather than an esthetic or structural study of literature and art or a narration of historical events, we shall fall into the error of those critics who accused him of omitting matters he never intended to deal with. In this aspect only, i.e., in his ultimate goal rather than in the method used, it may be said that Taine's interest was primarily psychological.

I *Taine's Achievements*

The consequences of this reversal of emphasis in criticism profoundly affected that entire discipline. The artistic work no longer occupied a sovereign status with historical and social conditions serving as accessories to fill out the portrait of the artist; in Taine's method the work of art constitutes the most powerful means of depicting the spirit of an age or the character of a race. Thus the literary critic becomes a literary historian in the fullest sense of the word. Beyond that, Taine attempted to depersonalize criticism by providing it with a scientific basis that would replace personal whim or taste by a more objective procedure.

That he was a pioneer in scientific criticism few will deny. No one before him, not even Sainte-Beuve, had ever attempted such a

rigorous program of applying the methods and laws of the physical
sciences to the study of humanistic subjects. In view of the enormous difficulties involved, not only in having no previous experience to fall back upon but also in facing the opposition of academic authorities and of customary prejudice, Taine's lasting and
valid contributions far outweigh those attempts in which he was
less successful. His articles on Balzac and Stendhal rank among
the classics in criticism on the two great novelists, passages from
La Fontaine and His Fables continue to appear in French text-
books, and his prefaces to the *Critical and Historical Essays* along
with the famous introduction to the *History of English Literature*
constitute milestones in critical theory. The last-mentioned work
represents the most successful illustration of his ambitious theory
which combined philosophy, history, literature, and psychology in
order to define the English character through the literary history of
that nation. Aside from brilliant chapters on Shakespeare, Milton,
Byron, Macaulay, and Carlyle, Taine proved that a literary history
can be more than a dreary succession of sketchy biographies and
summaries of works.

In his art criticism Taine pursued still further the idea that the
artistic creation is an expression of the society in which it was
produced, thus pioneering a work in the sociology of art. The portion of his *Lectures on Art* devoted to Italy provides the best example of this type of criticism. The sections on Greek art and
especially the one on art in the Netherlands combine sociological,
historical, and esthetic criticism with the tripartite theory of race,
milieu, and moment in Taine's most mature critical work. The
theoretical discussion of the nature and the production of artistic
works has lost none of its validity today, nor has the *Ideal in Art*
except for the questionable criterion concerning the beneficence
of character.

Where Taine did not succeed, we should look first to his own
personality before seeking flaws in his method. In his writings on
French literature of the seventeenth century and on the French
Revolution powerful tensions between his emotions and his method arose. Taine was obviously not the calm, disinterested sort of
researcher best suited to apply a scientific method and, although he
was both generous and tolerant, on some matters he displayed an
inflexible attitude. Curiously enough for a man who admitted to a

mind both Latin and Classical, he violently opposed these two traits in literature and political philosophy, preferring definitely minds that were Germanic and depictions that were at the same time individual and violent in emotional intensity. Pointing out that he was seeking psychological information in art and that he disliked the Classical spirit which posits abstract principles while eschewing experimentation, explains the attitudes of the critic, but not the inner complexity of the man. When we add to this the stylistic tension between a scientific thought and a lively, imagistic rendition of it, then every page written by Taine can be viewed as a personal struggle.

II   *Taine's Influence*

From 1857 until his death Taine, along with Renan, exerted more influence on French thought than any other writer. Two generations were so completely under his sway that only adherence or opposition to his doctrines seemed to be possible. Paul Bourget and Maurice Barrès were his most immediate intellectual descendants. Those influenced by his critical theories form an impressive group extending from J. J. Jusserand and Louis Cazamian[2] to Ferdinand Brunetière,[3] to I. A. Richards[4] and, in the United States, to Edward Eggleston and William Dean Howells[5] as well as to V. L. Parrington and Granville Hicks.[6] Even Albert Guérard, Sr., who felt a sort of love-hate for Taine, used race, milieu and moment in writing of the relationship between literature and society.[7] In art criticism, his most famous successor, Elie Faure, is indebted to Taine in his treatment of Rubens, Flemish and Dutch painting.[8] Rather than continue citing a long list of names, it may be said that any critic who draws in a large measure on disciplines other than the art medium itself, be it history, sociology, psychology, philosophy or any of the sciences, derives in a general way from Taine. Such critics need of course not adopt Taine's psychology or his social or historical views, yet by bringing to bear on criticism scientific and historical factors they are pursuing the road traced by Taine. The result assigns to Taine some rather strange bedfellows, since most psychological critics have been Freudians[9] and most sociological critics Marxists.

The influence of Taine has varied according to the intellectual prestige enjoyed by science as a problem solver. The critic himself can hardly be said to have profited to the maximum during his lifetime from the favorable position he occupied in France. Having devoted himself to historical works during the last twenty years of his life while practically abandoning literary and art criticism, he failed to play the predominant role that should have been rightfully his in French Naturalism. More than that, his personal tastes caused him to assume a rather negative attitude toward those writers who were his most legitimate heirs, in particular toward Emile Zola. A rather aristocratic and Classical sense of the limits of good taste and an increasing moral concern expressed clearly in the beneficence of character criterion in *The Ideal in Art,* veiled Taine's judgment of the Naturalists. In a letter to Anatole France, upon the publication of the latter's novel *The Crime of Sylvestre Bonnard* (1881), the critic gave vent to his objections: "Compensate us for the many contemporary talents led astray by the imitation of painting, by a taste for bad smells, by the conscious admiration of popular or bourgeois platitudes, disciples of Henri Monnier and of Courbet, and who, under the pretext of truth and direct rendition, will inspire in us disgust for life and horror of literature."[10]

Professor John C. Lapp has revealed, by means of their correspondence, that Taine showed an interest in Zola's early works and that he offered advice to the young writer which seems to have influenced Zola's conception of the *Rougon-Macquart* series of novels by presenting a wider social background and more balanced, antithetical characters,[11] but this correspondence stopped in 1875. Zola's name figures neither among the writers he considers promising in 1884 (Daudet, Maupassant, and Bourget) nor among the great living writers in 1887 (Emile Augier, Alexander Dumas the Younger, and Flaubert, in *Madame Bovary*).[12] It is an everlasting pity that the author of epoch-making articles on Balzac and Stendhal never wrote a printed line about Zola.

The great novelist was both aware of, and puzzled by, the attitude of Taine whose humble disciple he had declared himself to be in 1866. In an interview published in the *Figaro* the day after Taine's death (March 6, 1893), Zola declared: "There was a literary misunderstanding between us. I think he did not particularly like what I was writing and that always distressed me. I presented my candidature for the French Academy and he never supported me. Something, I know not what, separated us."

Just as Sainte-Beuve had misjudged most of his contemporaries, so Taine, who had rehabilitated the two great novelists mistreated by Sainte-Beuve, displayed little understanding for the most important literary movements of his critical career, since he felt also little sympathy for Baudelaire, Verlaine and the Symbolists.[13]

Not only the development of literary movements but the mood of the times as well turned against Taine's philosophy and critical method. In the 1890's a sharp reaction, not so much against science as such, but against scientism began to make itself felt. Taking stock, such critics as Brunetière concluded that Taine and Renan had been wrong in predicting that science would solve all problems. In a widely quoted article Brunetière spoke of "the bankruptcy of science" which had been unable to supply answers to the fundamental questions of man's origin and destiny.[14] This was, of course, a misstatement of Taine's position who had never promised that science would accomplish anything in particular by 1890; nevertheless, the opposition to scientism continued, along with an anti-rationalistic mood, well into the twentieth century, giving rise to such movements as Dadaism and Surrealism in France and Expressionism in Germany.

The most formidable attack against Taine and scientism came from Henri Bergson, the influential French philosopher who propounded a doctrine based on the "élan vital" and intuition. If there had been a misunderstanding between Zola and Taine, the same can be said for Taine and Bergson. Although miles apart on most matters, they shared a deep attachment to the intuitive capacity which both valued above the analytical one.[15] With the exception of Gustave Lanson,[16] the most notable French literary critics between the two world wars followed Bergson's lead and treated Taine with hostility. Albert Thibaudet, in a note of 1923, declared that Taine's ambitious constructions were by then "empty halls, unfurnished, humid, scarcely inhabitable." And he added insult to injury by describing Taine as a great orator,[17] the very blame the historian of English literature had pinned on those he wanted to denigrate. The anti-Taine campaign reached its climax in Fernand Baldensperger's judgment that "it has been necessary, in a great number of particular cases, to take the path opposite to

Taine's in order to achieve at least some critical approximations. . . .
French thought has resisted, thanks to a profound understanding
of the problems at stake, the theoretical intoxication to which
people fell prey only too easily at a time when Science seemed to
promise the solution of all problems."[18]

The evolution of scientific philosophy has not entirely worked
in Taine's favor, either. The problem is not that great strides have
not been made in the various sciences but rather that most matters Taine was concerned with (physiology, psychology, genetics)
have turned out to be far more complex than he had anticipated,
so that his relatively simple formulas concerning master faculty,
race, and milieu need at present to be expressed in complicated
equations the end of which is not yet in sight. In spite of the amaz-
ing progress in the sciences, J. Bronowski, a distinguished mathe-
matician who joins the "two cultures," states: "The laws of nature
cannot be formulated as an axiomatic, deductive, formal and un-
ambiguous system which is also complete. . . . The theorems of
Gödel and Tarski make it evident that this ideal is hopeless."[19]
It should be noted, however, that this is merely a summary of the
present state of scientific and logical development, and not the
last word to be said on the subject.

In the past twenty years a more favorable climate for the diffu-
sion of Taine's ideas has developed. Not only have the Bergsonian
critics lost ground, in their turn, but an increasing trend toward
scientific criticism of one sort or another can be observed. On the
one hand, the use of psychology and psychiatry in criticism continues to find strong adherents. In France the movement called the
"new criticism," which includes such critics as Roland Barthes,
Jean-Paul Weber, and Charles Mauron, draws not only on psychiatry but on linguistics and anthropology as well. On the other
hand, sociology serves as the basic tool for the Marxist critics,
both in the Soviet Union and elsewhere. But here a real dilemma
presents itself. Most of the critics involved necessarily hold political convictions opposed to those of Taine. While Balzac, a conservative if ever there was one, has found favor in Soviet Russia
due to his exposure of social ills, it is very difficult for liberal
critics to accept as their predecessor the public prosecutor of the
French Revolution and of the socialistic state. Yet, despite radical
differences in their conclusions, the Marxist critics posit a basic

view which is scarcely more than a variation of Taine's principle that great authors express their society, the difference being that Marxist critics replace "society" by "social class."

While some of these critics recognize Taine's contribution to sociological criticism and merely accuse him of not having "acceded to the truths of Marx,"[20] others ignore him altogether. Thus Lucien Goldmann has accomplished the feat of writing the following without so much as mentioning the name of Taine: "It often happens that the mode of behavior which enables us to understand a particular work is not that of the author himself, but that of a whole social group; and when the work with which we are concerned is of particular importance, this behavior is that of a whole social class."[21] And elsewhere, M. Goldmann states: "The great writer is precisely the exceptional individual who succeeds in creating in a certain field, that of the literary work (or pictorial, conceptual, musical, etc.), an imaginary, coherent or almost rigorously coherent universe whose structure corresponds to the one toward which the whole of the group tends; as for the work, it is . . . as much more mediocre or more important as its structure differs from or approaches the rigorous coherence."[22] One can, of course, not always choose one's spiritual ancestors any more than one's genetic forebears, but it is no easier to deny the former than the latter. Under the circumstances it is, however, not entirely clear whether Taine has been the victim of a conspiracy of silence or of ignorance.

Without going so far as to call Taine the father of present-day structuralism, it is safe to state that he pointed the way for the practitioners of that movement, namely, to arrive at the most basic structures in a system whose elements are interdependent. One is immediately reminded of Taine's pronouncement that "moral matters, as physical matters, have dependencies and conditions" upon reading the four requirements Claude Lévi-Strauss sets up for a structural system: "(1) A structure has the character of a system. It consists of elements such that any kind of modification of one entails a modification in all the others. (2) Every model belongs to a group of transformations each of which corresponds to a model of the same family so that the total of these transformations constitutes a group of models. (3) The properties indicated above enable us to foresee in what manner the model will react in case

one of its elemênts is modified. (4) The model must be so constituted that its functioning can account for all the observed facts."[23]

Even if Taine's fortune has undergone the vicissitudes of time
and fashion, he can be opposed and disliked but not ignored by
historians and critics of art and literature. His work remains to
speak for him, and that work is gigantic, both in its ambitions
and in what its author realized. Few modern writers have so completely combined the two cultures, as C. P. Snow calls them (the
humanities and the sciences) as Taine, and his method informs, in
many variations, the courses on world literature and the history
of ideas which are enjoying an ever-growing popularity in American high schools and colleges.

The fact remains that the problems Taine raised and on which
he took a stand are still very much with us. Comparing the two
great French critics of the nineteenth century, René Wellek concludes: "From a modern point of view Taine seems much more
relevant than Sainte-Beuve: he raises more issues, more theories."[24] A summary of these issues and theories proves Professor
Wellek's point. Taine left us this heritage: He claimed: *(1)* that
the laws of the physical sciences apply to human affairs as well;
(2) that criticism need not be dictated by personal whim or good
taste but that it can be based on philosophical assumptions; *(3)*
that artistic works are not mere personal creations but express the
spirit of their times; *(4)* that the principal causes of artistic creations are master faculty, race, milieu, and moment, and that a
knowledge of these causes enables us to study an individual, an
age, a race or an entire civilization; *(5)* that the progress in the
various fields of science should be reflected in criticism through
the use of new instruments of observation; *(6)* he provided the
basic philosophy of the Naturalist movement in France and elsewhere; and *(7)* he wrote the pioneer essays on Balzac and Stendhal.

In evaluating Taine's achievements today it becomes apparent
that the frequently formulated judgment of Taine as an excellent
critic in spite of his philosophical assumptions and method is incorrect. Professor Doubrovsky renders Taine due justice by stating: "It is not despite his philosophy but because of it that Taine
will have contributed to the progress of modern criticism by his
quest for a clearly articulated and total explanation far more than
men like Lemaître or Faguet by their voluble impressionism."[25]

It is time to take leave of Taine. The person we have come to know is not a dry pedant but a man in his study surrounded by books and voluminous notes, communing, like a modern Faust, with Spinoza, Hegel and Stendhal, conjuring up before his nearsighted eyes entire epochs of the past: ancient Greece, the Italian Renaissance, the French Classical centuries, struggling to detect the hidden springs in a Michelangelo, a Rembrandt, a Shakespeare, turning his eyes inward to discover the meaning of the Ego, of perception, of imagination, of the narrow limits that separate sanity and insanity, reality and illusion; opening them again in horrified anger at the spectacle of men and women beheaded or marched up the steps of the guillotine by French revolutionaries. And as his logical mind orders the facts, sifts out the causes and explains their effects, these visions continue to haunt him while the historian, the philosopher, the psychologist and the critic whisper phrases into his ear which his artistic imagination transforms into a work of art.

Notes and References

Chapter One

1. *Essai sur Tite-Live* (Paris, 1904), p. 330.
2. *History of English Literature,* transl. by H. Van Laun (New York, 1872), II, 339. Hereafter referred to as *History.*
3. The only "scandal" in Taine's life seems to have been his association with Camille Selden. Taine knew her from about 1858 to 1868, the year of his marriage. In her Memoirs (published in the *Revue Germanique* (1906), pp. 518 ff.) Camille Selden, eighteen years after their break, accuses Taine of having abandoned her and draws a quite uncomplimentary portrait of him; yet Taine probably aided her in the writing of her novels and gave her publicity in two articles he wrote about her in the *Journal des Débats.* A certain Dr. Michaut launched a posthumous and incoherent attack against Taine in *Etudes psychologiques. L'Amour d'un saint laï'que. Un crime de Hippolyte Taine* (Paris, 1905), but the author is so obviously prejudiced that his statements cannot be taken very seriously. The Brothers Goncourt, who knew Taine primarily from the literary dinners at the Magny Restaurant, portray the critic in a very unfavorable light. They show him as pedantic, sometimes salacious, and accuse him of having married his wife for her dowry. But then the Goncourts rarely had a kind word for anybody.
4. *Journal des Débats,* March 16, 1893.
5. *H. Taine: Sa Vie et sa correspondance* (Paris, 1902-1907), 4 vols. The editors were Taine's widow and André Chevrillon, his nephew. English: *Life and Letters* of H. Taine (New York, 1902-1908), 3 vols. Vol. 1-2, transl. by Mrs. R. L. Devonshire; Vol. 3 abridged and transl. by E. Sparvel-Bayly. Hereafter referred to as *Life and Letters.* Since this translation is incomplete, letters will be identified by addressee and date.
6. By the Comte de Vogüé, in *Journal des Débats,* March 6, 1893.

Also in Vogüé's *Devant le siecle* (Paris, 1896), p. 294.

7. Vogüé, in *Journal des Débats*, March 6, 1893.

8. Emile Faguet, *Politiques et moralistes du XIXe siècle* (Paris, 1900), p. 250.

9. Gabriel Monod, *Les Maîtres de l'histoire: Renan, Taine, Michelet* (Paris, 1894), p. 153.

10. Lucien Anatole Prévost-Paradol, in Octave Gérard, *Prévost-Paradol* (Paris, 1894), p. 149.

11. Jules Lemaître, *Les Contemporains* (Paris, 1891), III, 343.

12. *L'Avenir de la science,* written in 1848 but published only in 1890.

13. *Origines de l'alchimie* (Paris, 1885), p. 5.

14. It should be noted that Taine exposed his scientific method as early as 1858, in his *Critical and Historical Essays.*

15. In literature the decline of French Romanticism is marked by the failure of Victor Hugo's ambitious drama *Les Burgraves* (1843).

16. In *The Nineteenth Century Classical Philosophers,* discussed in Chapter 2, below.

17. *Le Temps,* March 12, 1893.

18. *L'Evolution des genres dans l'histoire de la littérature* (Paris, 1898), I, 246. Among the many other admirers of Taine was Friedrich Nietzsche, who considered Taine and the famous Renaissance historian Jakob Burckhardt the only men in Europe capable of understanding his books. (See Nietzsche's letters to Baron von Seydlitz, dated Nice, October 26, 1886, and to Jakob Burckhardt, dated Nice, November 14, 1887.)

19. *Life and Letters,* I, 12-16.

20. Founded in 1808 by Napoleon I with the object of training young professors who had to sign an agreement obliging them to teach for ten years.

21. Edmond About (1828-1885), journalist and novelist; Francisque Sarcey (1827-1899), drama critic of *Le Temps*; Edouard de Suckau (1828-1867) obtained first place in the *agrégation* examination of 1851 in which Taine was unsuccessful; Lucien Anatole Prévost-Paradol (1829-1870), Taine's closest friend until their different political views led to a break around 1864. An ardent liberal, Prévost-Paradol eventually accepted an ambassadorial post from Napoleon III. Realizing the gravity of his about-face, he committed suicide in 1870, shortly after arriving in Washington.

22. *A Tour Through the Pyrenees* (1855). Other travel books describe trips to Italy, England and the French provinces. Taine used to document himself very carefully before setting out on a trip and he has been charged with efforts to confirm his preconceived opinions.

Frequently the first-hand information gathered was utilized by him in his work, as in the *History of English Literature* (1864) and in his books on art in Italy and in the Netherlands. He possessed a thorough knowledge of English.

23. Especially *La Revue de l'Instruction Publique, Le Journal des Débats,* and *La Revue des Deux Mondes.*

24. Particularly a reference to Bossuet: "Bossuet did not add much to Livy. He summed up history in a large sense and a grandiose style, but as if written for children, and he raced through it in a great hurry." (Letter to Prévost-Paradol, June 3, 1854).

25. Marcelin, in *La Vie parisienne,* February 18, 1865.

26. Paul Bourget, *Essais de psychologie contemporaine* (Paris, 1885), p. 183.

27. Letter to Prévost-Paradol, May 1, 1849.

28. Letter to Mme. H. Taine, June 28, 1873.

29. Letter to Joseph Hornung, November 19, 1875.

30. *Journeys through France, Being Impressions of the Provinces,* anonymous transl. (New York, 1897), p. 70.

31. Paul Bourget (1852-1935), novelist and essay writer who depicted Taine in his novel *Le Disciple* (1889); Eugène Melchior de Vogüé (1848-1910) is best known for *Le Roman russe* (1886); Gaston Paris (1839-1903) was a famous philologist and medieval scholar; José-Maria de Hérédia (1842-1905) is best known for his perfect sonnets in *Les Trophées* (1893); the brothers Berthelot were scientists; and Ernest Lavisse (1842-1922) was a famous historian.

32. Letter to Prévost-Paradol, May 1, 1849.

33. *Life and Letters,* III, 253.

34. Letter to Georges Lyon, December 9, 1891. Elsewhere (*Ancient Régime,* p. 209), in one of his striking phrases, he calls religion "a metaphysical poem accompanied by faith."

35. Paul Bourget, in *Le Disciple* (1889), describes a philosopher, Adrien Sixte, who resembles Taine in many ways, and whose disciple Greslou is led into amorality and despair in his efforts to apply the principles of his master to his life. Taine was greatly disturbed by what he considered a dangerously partial exposition of his views. Maurice Barrès went even further by paying homage to him in a chapter ("L'Arbre de M. Taine") in his novel *Les Déracinés.* Both Bourget and Barrès became opponents of Dreyfus during the famous trial.

36. *The Modern Regime,* transl. by J. Durand (New York, 1890-1894), II, 123.

37. H. F. Amiel, *Amiel's Journal,* transl. by Mrs. Humphrey Ward (New York, 18—), p. 232.

38. *Life and Letters,* II, 217; translation altered.
39. *Ibid.,* II, 219; translation altered.
40. Georges Brandès, *Essais choisis* (Paris, 1914), p. 95.

Chapter Two

1. Letter to Georges Lyon, December 9, 1891.
2. His student notebooks, partly reproduced in André Chevrillon. *Taine: Formation de sa pensée* (Paris, 1932), pp. 385-409; and in S. J. Kahn, *Science and Aesthetic Judgment; A Study in Taine's Critical Method* (London, 1953), pp. 209-27; *The Nineteenth Century Classical Philosophers;* the chapter on Stuart Mill in *History,* II, 477-517; some parts of *On Intelligence,* and portions of his two prefaces to *Critical and Historical Essays* constitute Taine's entire philosophical writings.
3. Taine himself referred increasingly to "history" and "historians" in his theoretical writings. Cf. *Essais de critique et d'histoire* (Paris, 1904), pp. xi-xii, xxvii, (hereafter referred to as *Essais*), and *Lectures on Art,* transl. by J. Durand (New York, 1896), I, 195-96.
4. He apologized for not having exposed an entire philosophical system, in *Les Philosophes classiques du XIXᵉ siècle* (Paris, 1905), p. i, referred to hereafter as *Phils. class.;* again, in his preface to the second edition of his *Essais,* he insists that his is a method, not a philosophical system. (*Essais,* xiii.)
5. For philosophical influences on Taine, see D. D. Rosca, *L'Influence de Hegel sur Taine théoricien de la connaissance et de l'art* ((Paris, 1928); Chevrillon, *op. cit.;* Kahn, *op. cit.;* and D. G. Charlton, *Positivist Thought in France during the Second Empire, 1852-1870* (Oxford, 1959), pp. 127-58.
6. Taine's major criticism of Descartes and of the French Classical spirit is the a priori approach of mathematics and a neglect of experience and experiment.
7. *Life and Letters,* I, 91; translation slightly altered.
8. The original title was *Les Philosophes français du XIXᵉ siècle.* The definitive title appeared in the third edition (1868) in which the biting tone is somewhat softened.
9. *Phils. class.,* p. 59.
10. "Abstraction" here means abstract terms that have no basis in fact, and not the process of abstraction. (Cf. chapter on Stuart Mill, in *History,* II, 506-12.)
11. *Phils. class.,* pp. 291-92; Kahn, pp. 47-48.
12. *History,* II, 494-95; *On Intelligence,* transl. by T. D. Haye (New York, 1889), II, 230. This view is inspired by Spinoza's proposition that "the order and connection of things is the same as the order and

connection of ideas." (*Ethics*, Part II, Prop. vii.)

13. Implied in this view is Hegel's principle which sees in the "Idea" the generative factor and the goal of the universe. One difference between Hegel and Taine is that the former is certain he knows the universal cause, while the latter believes it can eventually be discovered.

14. *Phils. class.*, pp. ix, 351. In his student notebooks Taine repeatedly wrote Aristotle's definition: to know means knowing the cause.

15. *Ibid.*, pp. 323, 324.

16. *Ibid.*, pp. 326-27.

17. *Ibid.*, pp. 342-43.

18. *Ibid.*, pp. 350-51.

19 This illustration of cause has been attacked, since nutrition is not anterior to, does not engender, the digestive organs and functions, and Taine has been accused of confusing *efficient* and *final* causes.

20. *Ibid.*, p. 363.

21. *Essais*, p. xiii.

22. *Ibid.*, p. iii.

23. La Mettrie published a work by that title in 1747.

24. *Essai sur Tite-Live*, p. vii.

25. *History*, I, 6. Constantly accused of equating vice and virtue to chemical products, Taine had to explain over and over again that he was referring to moral and psychological products, that moral dispositions, whether good or bad, "have as their causes other moral dispositions that are simpler and easier to distinguish." (Letter to Director of *Journal des Débats*, December 19, 1872.)

26. Taine incorrectly refers to this theory as "the connection of characters." (*Essais*, p. xxiv n.)

27. *Ibid.*, pp. xvii-xviii.

27a. *Les Philosophes français du XIXe siècle* (Paris, 1857), p. 354. This phrase is omitted in later editions.

28. Letter to E. Havet, April 29, 1864.

29. *History*, I, 14.

30. Letter to Jules Lemaître, March 28, 1887.

31. *History*, II, 407.

32. Letter to Théophile Cart, October 26, 1884.

33. André Chevrillon, *Portrait de Taine: Souvenirs* (Paris, 1958), p. 124.

34. *Essais*, pp. xiv-xv. Elsewhere Taine summarizes his research in an oft-quoted phrase: "In little, well-selected, important, significant facts, stated with full details and minutely noted, we find at present the materials of every science." (*On Intelligence*, I, vii.)

35. *Essais*, p. xix.

36. Taine always felt that the reader should not be bored with details of the writer's research difficulties. "In the historian there is the critic who checks the facts, the scholar who gathers them together, the philosopher who explains them; but all these characters remain hidden behind the poet who tells the story. They whisper into his ear all his words but do not speak themselves. . . . Abstractions, compilations, controversies must be melted into a work of art inspired by imagination." (*Essai sur Tite-Live,* p. 357.)

37. Among others, Alvin A. Eustis, *Hippolyte Taine and the Classical Genius* (Berkeley and Los Angeles, 1951), pp. 42-43.

38. *History,* II, 502.

39. Monod, p. 154.

40. Gottfried Wilhelm von Leibnitz, *On Method: Preface to the General Science* (1677).

41. Taine accused Kant of taking as starting point of his critique that there are synthetic judgments a priori; Taine's rebuttal to this is that they are all latent analytical judgments. (Letter to Ernest Renan, September 9, [1872].) By 1876 he discounted Kant as "an overrated philosopher none of whose theories stand up nowadays and who has been relegated by Spencer, Stuart Mill and positive psychology to the rear of Hume, Condillac, even of Spinoza," (Letter to Ernest Renan, June 3, 1876.)

42. Letter to Prévost-Paradol, November 16, 1851.

43. *History,* II, 516-17.

44. André Chevrillon, "La jeunesse de Taine," *Revue de Paris* (July 15, 1902), p. 30.

45. He speculated that the law of the conservation of energy might be one of those supreme laws. Cf. *De l'Intelligence* (Paris, 1948), I, 10. (Not in the English translation.)

46. *Phils. class.,* pp. 368-71.

47. *De l'Intelligence,* II, 462-63; *On Intelligence,* 288-89. The English translation, based on the first edition, is not as explicit as later French editions.

48. *On Intelligence,* I, vii.

49. An interesting testimony on the difference between hallucination and poetic imagination is provided by Gustave Flaubert: "Don't confuse the mental vision of the artist with the state of laboring under hallucination. I know both states perfectly; there is a chasm between them. In strict hallucination there is always fear; you feel your personality escaping you; you think you are about to die. In poetic vision, on the contrary, there is joy; it is something which enters into you. It is none the less true that one loses consciousness of where one is." (*Ibid.,* I, 262.)

50. R. S. Peters (ed.), *Brett's History of Psychology* (London and New York, 1962), p. 494. Taine's influence in psychology did not cease with the general acceptance of views by Freud and others. As late as 1936, Jean-Paul Sartre, in *L'Imagination* (Paris, 1936, pp. 24-25), launched a vigorous attack against *On Intelligence,* accusing Taine of using a deductive method, of presenting no concrete descriptions and constructing a logical rather than a scientific edifice by making uncontrolled principles determine in advance the results of experiments.

51. Taine had intended to publish his theory on will but was unable to complete it. His notes have been published in the *Revue de Philosophie* (November, 1900), pp. 442-80.

52. See note 12 in this chapter.

53. See note 41 in this chapter.

54. *On Intelligence,* I, 91. Compare this with Freud's explanation of amnesia in his *Collected Papers* (London, 1940), 2nd edition, I, 32-33; 267.

55. *On Intelligence,* I, 117; translation slightly altered.

56. *Ibid.,* II, 2; I, 240-41.

57. *Ibid.,* I, 266.

58. *Ibid.,* II, 120.

59. *Notes on Paris,* transl. by John Austin Stevens (New York, 1879), p. 280.

60. *History,* I, 240-41.

61. *The Ancient Regime,* transl. by John Durand (London, 1881), p. 238.

62. *The French Revolution,* transl. by J. Durand (New York, 1878-1885), I, 53.

63. *Derniers essais de critique et d'histoire* (Paris, 1894), pp. 116-17.

Chapter Three

1. *Essais,* pp. vii-viii.

2. Elsewhere Taine placed Sainte-Beuve among the five writers who have contributed most to the knowledge of human nature and society since Montesquieu. The others: Balzac, Stendhal, Guizot, and Renan. (Letter to Editor of *Journal des Débats,* March 3, 1887.)

3. *Derniers essais de critique et d'histoire,* pp. 59-60.

4. Article on Camille Selden's *L'Esprit des femmes dans notre temps,* in *Journal des Débats,* January 26, 1865.

5. Quoted in Bourget, p. 224.

6. *Life and Letters,* II, 219; translation altered.

7. Most guilty of this attitude have been many of Taine's friends

and admirers who could not bring themselves to accept his philosophical views. Among these are Victor Giraud, *Essai sur Taine, son oeuvre et son influence* (Paris, 1902), p. 132; Daniel Mornet in *Cahiers ardennais* (November 2, 1928), p. 54; Brandès, pp. 94-95; and Marcelino Menéndez y Pelayo, *Historia de las ideas estéticas en España* (Madrid, 1889), IV (2), 341.

8. The concept of the master faculty or ruling passion is, of course, a very old one. Giraud, p. 41, n. 1, assigns it for no obvious reason to Friedrich Schlegel's *Philosophy of History* (translated into French in 1836). Yet it is already implied in the humoral psychology of medicine and finds its strongest expression prior to Taine in Pope's *Essay on Man*, II, vv. 142 ff., who, in turn, may be indebted to Bacon's essay "On Empire" and Montaigne's essay "On Repentance".

9. *History*, I, 17.

10. Letter to Cornelis de Witt, July 24, 1853.

11. *Essais*, p. v.

12. *Ibid.*, p. ix.

13. This is the first time this term was applied to a writer. Taine's influence on the later literary movement of Naturalism was considerable.

14. *Nouveaux essais de critique et d'histoire* (Paris, 1905), pp. 59-60, hereafter referred to as *Nouveaux essais*. This is the first version of the "vice and virtue" phrase which will reoccur in the Introduction to *History*, I, 6.

15. *Nouveaux essais*, p. 81.

16. Taine does not consider the fact that Balzac was born in the provinces, at Tours, and did not come to Paris until he was fifteen. His tendency to depict Paris as the mysterious and wicked capital has been pointed out by more recent critics.

17. See *Phils. class.*, pp. 368-71, quoted above, p. 43.

18. *Nouveaux essais*, p. 94.

19. *Ibid.*, p. 55.

20. *Life and Letters*, II, 159-60.

21. Stendhal, *Histoire de la peinture en Italie* (Paris, 1924), II. 34-35, 75.

22. See his letter to Prévost-Paradol, December 30, 1851.

23. Stendhal, *Romans et Nouvelles* (Paris: Gallimard, 1952), I. 768-69.

24. *Nouveaux essais*, p. 194.

25. Letter to Paul Bourget, July 30, 1883. *Lucien Leuwen*, then called *The Green Huntsman (Le Chasseur Vert)* he read twenty times. (Letter to Mme. H. Taine, May, 1891.) In the course of time Taine

lost sympathy for Julien Sorel, finally calling him odious. (Letter to Vogüé, June 8, 1886.)

26. *Nouveaux essais*, p. 223. Taine had already described Balzac as a "superior mind" in praising his ability to present synthetic views (*Ibid.*, 80) but this had not been intended as representing Balzac's master faculty.

27. *Ibid.*, p. 231.

28. *Essais*, p. 209.

29. *Ibid.*, p. 113.

30. *Derniers essais*, p. 132.

31. *Nouveaux essais*, p. 151.

32. *The Ancient Regime*, p. 266.

33. *Ibid.*, p. 221.

34. *Ibid.*, p. 262.

35. Taine never claimed that his method was capable of explaining genius (see pp. 85-86 below). The final answer to this question is likely to be a genetic one and would require the breaking of the genetic code, but this only strengthens Taine's position that progress depends on the invention of better instruments of observation.

36. On this matter, see Eustis, pp. 24-25, 27. Some of these inconsistencies can be explained by the effect Taine wanted to produce (e.g. Racine is used to demonstrate how unsuccessful the English Restoration theater was in attempting to imitate the French Classical theater), but others pose a more serious problem.

37. See *Life and Letters*, II, 217, quoted above, pp. 25-26.

38. For an explanation of the method, see above, pp. 39-40.

39. *History*, I, 508-9.

40. *The Ancient Regime*, p. 187.

41. *Nouveaux essais*, p. 111.

42. In a study of 1851 on Descartes' method, Taine criticized the argument "I think therefore I am" as being general and abstract. "One does not think purely and simply, one thinks something; so we see that Descartes' principle is not first, for abstract perceptions come only after concrete ones, and general perceptions only after particular ones. Now, it is a great defect in a principle not to be first." (Chevrillon, *Taine: Formation de sa pensée*, pp. 394-95.)

43. *History*, I, 340.

44. For example, he felt that, for style, the seventeenth-century writers had no equals. "Aside from Pascal, among our Classical writers La Fontaine is the first for simple effects and La Bruyère for complex effects. The list of our masters begins with Calvin and Montaigne and ends with the seventeenth century." (Letter to G. Saint-René Tail-

landier, November 21, 1890.)

45. *Nouveaux essais*, p. 153.

45a. Charles Mauron, in *L'Inconscient dans l'oeuvre et la vie de Racine* (Paris, 1957), p. 265, explains this apparent discrepancy in Racine's life in terms of present-day views: "A life without apparent passion is in no way incompatible with an unconscious full of torment. On the contrary, the most neurotic and oddly the most obsessed men are those who lead socially acceptable surface lives but which àre narcissistic and devoid of real love for others."

46. *Essais*, pp. 248-49.

47. *Nouveaux essais*, p. 162.

48. It is worthy of note that Racine has been the touchstone in the current controversy about the so-called New Criticism in France. See Raymond Picard, *Nouvelle Critique ou nouvelle imposture* (Paris, 1965).

49. *Nouveaux essais*, p. 122. Molière was so frequently accused of having used contemporary models that he had to issue a formal denial in *The Versailles Impromptu*.

50. *Ibid.*, p. 138.

51. *Ibid.*, p. 147.

52. *Ibid.*, p. 129.

53. *La Fontaine et ses fables* (Paris, 1905), pp. 344-45.

54. *Ibid.*, p. 18.

55. "It is interesting to see the difficulty the Gallic spirit in La Fontaine had to free itself from the public current that was leading it elsewhere. The reigning taste pushed people toward brilliant wit, eloquence, Classical rules, imitation of the Latins. . . . In this artificial and correct country he is not at ease." (*La Fontaine et ses fables*, p. 39.)

56. *Ibid.*, p. 319.

57. *History*, II, 105-6.

58. *Essais*, p. 218.

59. *La Fontaine et ses fables*, p. 158.

60. Racine's psychological insights have been the subject of recent studies by Martin Turnell, *The Classical Moment: Studies of Corneille, Molière and Racine* (London, 1947), pp. 133-241; and Roland Barthes, *On Racine*, transl. by Richard Howard (New York, 1964).

61. *Essais*, p. 228. Taine severely criticized Flaubert's style, predicting the novelist's descriptions would be unintelligible in a hundred years. "I continue to think that his state of mind is not transmissible by writing, but only by painting; he answers that such is the state of his mind and of all modern minds." (*Life and Letters*, II, 195.)

62. *La Fontaine et ses fables*, p. 69. This had been previously point-

ed out by René Wellek, *A History of Modern Criticism, 1750-1950* (New Haven and London, 1965), IV, 48-49.

Chapter Four

1. Letter to Edouard de Suckau, October 9, 1857.
2. *Ibid.*
3. *On Intelligence*, II, 138.
4. *Lectures on Art*, I, 216-17.
5. *History*, I, 11.
6. In the discussion of the seventeenth century and Racine, below in Chapter 3.
7. *Lectures on Art*, I, 104.
8. Taine's concept of "moment" has given rise to divergent views. While Brunetière, I, 262-63, considers moment the most important of the three primordial factors, Winthrop H. Rice, "The Meaning of Taine's *Moment*," *Romanic Review* XXX (1939), 272-79, sees it as the product of the other two forces and hence of less or almost no importance: as if one were to say that water is made up of H_2O, and water. Both of these interpretations seem extreme. Taine's examples establish moment as an equal partner with the other two forces by describing it as a factor that can be accounted for neither by race nor by milieu, both of which are relatively static. It is the experience contained in the dynamic cultural heritage at a given time and the artist's awareness of it.
9. *History*, I, 14.
10. Chevrillon, *Taine: Formation de sa pensée*, p. 338.
11. Taine acknowledged Montesquieu and Stendhal among his predecessors. Others include Thomas Warton. *History of English Poetry* (1774), Louis de Bonald, and Mme. de Staël.
12. *History*, I, 18-19; translation slightly altered.
13. Especially in the added fifth volume on contemporary authors, the omission of the Brownings, Ruskin, and George Eliot.
14. *La Fontaine et ses fables*, p. 344.
15. *Essais*, p. 93.
16. Letter to Sainte-Beuve, May 30, 1864.
17. *Lectures on Art*, II, 187.
18. *Ibid.*, II, 187-88.
19. *History*, II, 450. It should be noted that Taine does not strictly adhere to racial divisions, since Macaulay, an Englishman, illustrates the Latin turn of mind while the French historian Michelet possesses a Germanic mentality. Taine, who attributed the gift of synthesis pri-

marily to German thinkers, is here close to Sainte-Beuve's idea of the family of minds, which was not arranged according to races but composed of individuals across races and time.

20. *Ibid.*, II, 176.

21. *Ibid.*, I, 295.

22. *Ibid.*, I, 310-11, 340.

23. John S. White, "Taine on Race and Genius," *Social Research* (February, 1943), p. 96.

24. *History*, I, 320.

25. *Ibid.*, I, 338, 339-40.

26. *Ibid.*, II, 274 (pp. 273-88 are inserted by error in vol. II).

27. *Ibid.*, II, 27. Taine's purpose here is obviously not to praise Racine but to bury the English Restoration playwrights.

28. *Ibid.*, II, 212.

29. *Ibid.*, II, 189.

30. *Ibid.*, I, 274 (pp. 273-88 are inserted by error in vol. I).

31. *Ibid.*, I, 278.

32. *Ibid.*, II, 310-11.

33. *Ibid.*, II, 517.

34. *Ibid.*, II, 258, 262, 351, 349.

35. *Ibid.*, II, 365, 366.

36. *Ibid.*, II, 401.

37. *Ibid.*, I, 132.

38. Johan Huizinga, *The Waning of the Middle-Ages; A Study of the Forms of Life, Thought and Art in France and in the Netherlands in the XIVth and XVth Centuries* (London, 1924).

39. *History*, I, 111-12.

40. *Ibid.*, I, 144.

41. *Ibid.*, I, 154-55.

42. Albert Camus, *Discours de Suède* (Paris, 1958), pp. 37-38.

43. Already suggested by Emile Hennequin, *La Critique scientifique* (Paris, 1888), p. 139, in the formula: "A work will have an esthetic effect only on those who possess a mentality analogous or inferior to the one which has served to create the work and which can be deduced from it."

Chapter Five

1. H. Taine, *Italy: Florence and Venice,* transl. by J. Durand (New York, 1871), p. 130.

2. This is a collection of the lectures Taine gave at the Ecole des Beaux-Arts at Paris between 1863 and 1869, and consisting of the following: *The Philosophy of Art* (1865), *Philosophy of Art in Italy*

(1866), *The Ideal in Art* (1867), *Philosophy of Art in the Netherlands* (1868), *Philosophy of Art in Greece* (1869).

3. H. Taine, *Philosophie de l' Art* (Paris, 1964), pp. 11-14.

4. *Lectures on Art,* I, 75. Architecture and music, which are not imitative arts, are based on mathematical relationships.

5. Examples of representative characters are the ecstatic monk and the amorous knight in the Middle Ages, the perfect courtier in France in the seventeenth century, and, in the nineteenth century, the insatiable and sad Faust and Werther.

6. H. Taine, *Italy: Rome and Naples,* transl. by J. Durand (New York, 1870), p. 60.

7. *Italy: Florence and Venice,* p. 100.

8. *Lectures on Art,* II, 125-26.

9. *Ibid.,* II, 139-40.

10. Edmond Scherer, *Etudes sur la littérature contemporaine* (Paris, 1873), IV, 262.

11. This view is quite consistent with what Taine had stated in *History,* I, 132-33, quoted below, p. 96.

12. *Lectures on Art,* II, 131-32.

13. *Ibid.,* II, 415-16.

14. *Ibid.,* II, 465-66.

15. For Winckelmann's influence in France, and particularly on Gautier, see Raymond D. Giraud, "Winckelmann's Part in Gautier's Perception of Classical Beauty," *Yale French Studies,* No. 38 (1967), 172-82.

16. Certainly, Taine had read Lessing, but did he know the *Laokoon?* He mentions Lessing as a forerunner of his method in the Introduction to *History,* I, 4.

17. *Lectures on Art,* II, 308-11.

18. *Ibid.,* II, 234-35.

19. *Ibid.,* II, 226.

20. See Kahn, pp. 242-43, where an attempt is made to apply Taine's criteria to modern abstract art, specifically Picasso's "Guernica" mural.

21. No specific names are mentioned. We must assume that Taine is thinking of Spanish painters such as Goya, Velásquez and Murillo.

22. *Lectures on Art,* I, 273.

23. *Ibid.,* I, 279.

24. See *History,* II, 407, 401, quoted above on pp. 36 and 95-96 respectively. Even during his trip to Italy he declared himself sensitive "to the tragic and poignant sentiment of truth, the intensity of suffering vision, the audacious painting of human squalor and misery, . . . that is, to the paintings of Rembrandt." (*Italy: Rome and Naples,* p. v.)

25. Only four letters of the years 1865 and 1866 are contained in Taine's published correspondence. Somewhere during these years, between 1866 and 1868, he broke with the novelist Camille Selden and in 1868 he got married. It can be stated that henceforth Taine was no longer as unconcerned with country, family and morality as he had seemed to be at the time of writing *The Nineteenth Century Classical Philosophers*. In an unpublished Ph.D. dissertation, "H. Taine: The Neurotic" (University of Kentucky, 1949), pp. 268-69, Laura Jean McAdams attributes Taine's apparent change on moral judgments to a mellowing process that made him more benevolent toward man's sufferings as his admiration for blind and unjust nature diminished. See also Charles Picard, *H. Taine* (Paris, 1909), pp. 70-72.

Chapter Six

1. *Essai sur Tite-Live*, pp. 129, 131.
2. *Ancient Regime*, pp. 176, 179; translation altered.
3. Letter to G. Saint-René Taillandier, August 6, 1881. Taine was well aware that his approach involved the risk of omissions and errors, but he felt confident that future historians would correct these shortcomings.
4. *History*, II, 473-74.
5. Letter to Ernest Havet, March 24, 1878.
6. In Chapter 3, below.
7. *Ancient Regime*, p. 191.
8. *Ibid.*, p. 192.
9. *Ibid.*, p. 201; italics mine.
10. *The French Revolution*, I, 298.
11. *Ibid.*, II, 303; III, 351.
12. *Ibid.*, III, 39-40. For more sympathetic portrayals of the revolutionary mentality see George Rudé, *The Crowd in the French Revolution* (Oxford, 1959), especially chapters 12 and 13; and Richard Cobb, "Quelques aspects de la mentalité révolutionnaire," *Revue d'Histoire Moderne et Contemporaine*, VI (1959), 81-120.
13. *The French Revolution*, II, 352.
14. *Ibid.*, III, 136-37.
15. *cuistre* is one of those slow-burning insults in French that could still cause a duel. Originally the word described a low-paid tutor in a boarding school who would also serve on tables, but the term implies both pedantry and vulgarity. Taine, in bestowing this description on Robespierre, claims a *cuistre* results from the combination of being obtuse and a charlatan, "the hollow, inflated mind which, filled with words and imagining that these are ideas, revels in its own declamation and dupes itself that it may dictate to others." (*Ibid.*, III, 145.)

16. *Ibid.,* II, 22-23.

17. *Ibid.,* III, 189.

18. *Ibid.,* III, iii.

19. *Ancient Regime,* p. 251.

20. Thiers, Mignet, and Droz, all writing in the first quarter of the nineteenth century, were constitutional royalists, but the most widely read books on the French Revolution were produced in the 1840's by Lamartine, Michelet, and Louis Blanc, all of whom were ardent republicans opposed to the July Monarchy.

21. Quoted in Victor Giraud, pp. 273-74.

22. Peter Amann, "Taine, Tocqueville, and the Paradox of the Ancient Regime," *Romanic Review* LII (1961), 183-95, suggests that Taine had at first taken over Tocqueville's thesis that the downfall of the Ancient Regime was inevitable, but that, as the work progressed, he claimed it could have been saved by reforms.

23. G.-P. Gooch, *History and Historians of the Nineteenth Century* (London, 1920), p. 245.

24. *The French Revolution,* I, 303.

25. *Ibid.,* I, 116.

26. *Ibid.,* I, 145.

27. Armand E. Singer, "The Effect of the War of 1870 on the Development of Taine's Thought" (Unpublished Ph.D. dissertation, Duke University, 1943), p. 194.

28. *Vie et correspondance,* III, 325.

29. Paul Lacombe, *Taine historien et sociologue* (Paris, 1909); A. Aulard, *Taine historien de la Révolution française* (Paris, 1907).

30. Quoted in Gooch, p. 238.

Chapter Seven

1. Harry Levin, "Literature as an Institution," *Accent* (Spring, 1946), p. 159.

2. J. J. Jusserand, *Histoire littéraire du peuple anglais* (Paris, 1894); Louis Cazamian, *L'Evolution psychologique de la littérature en Angleterre* (Paris, 1920).

3. Although disagreeing on many points with Taine, Brunetière attempted to apply science to literary criticism in his theory of the evolution of genres.

4. I. A. Richards, *Principles of Literary Criticism* (London, 1924).

5. See Everett Carter, "Taine and American Realism," *Revue de Littérature comparée,* XXVI (1952), 357-64.

6. Levin, p. 162.

7. Albert Guérard, Sr., *Literature and Society* (Boston, 1935).

8. R. Wiarda, *Taine et la Hollande* (Paris, 1938), p. 279.

9. See, for example, Frederick J. Hoffman, *Freudianism and the Literary Mind* (Baton Rouge, La., 1945).

10. Quoted in Jeanne-Marie Pouquet, *Le Salon de Madame Caillavet* (Paris, n.d.), p. 63.

11. John C. Lapp, "Taine et Zola: Autour d'une correspondance," *Revue des Sciences humaines* (July-September, 1957), 319-26.

12. Letter to Georges Patinot, August 11, 1884; and letter to the Editor of *Journal des Débats,* March 3, 1887.

13. He appreciated Baudelaire's *Poems in Prose,* but confessed to little liking of the poet's *Flowers of Evil* (Letter to Bourget, November 24, 1881), and he advised his daughter not to read Verlaine and similar poets who "have the effect of hashish or of morphine on the mind." (Letter to his daughter, August, 1891.)

14. Ferdinand Brunetiére, "Après une visite au Vatican," *Revue les Deux Mondes,* CXXIII (January 1, 1895), 97-118.

15. See above, pp. 88-89.

16. Gustave Lanson, *Histoire de la littérature française* (Paris, 1903), pp. 1027-32.

17. Albert Thibaudet, *Réflexions sur la littérature* (Paris, 1938), I, 200.

18. Fernand Baldensperger, "L'Opposition française à l'esthétique de Taine," *Romanic Review,* XXXVI (1945), 131, 133.

19. J. Bronowski, "The Logic of the Mind," *American Scientist* (Spring-March, 1966), pp. 5, 4. The author explains Gödel's theorems, established in 1931, thus: "The first theorem says that any logical system which is not excessively simple (that is, which at least includes ordinary arithmetic) can express true assertions which nevertheless cannot be deduced from its axioms. And the second theorem says that the axioms in such a system, with or without additional truths, cannot be shown in advance to be free from hidden contradictions. In short, a logical system which has any richness can never be complete, yet cannot be guaranteed to be consistent." (*Ibid.,* p. 3.)

20. Stefan Morawski, "Les conceptions esthétiques de Taine," *La Pensée,* Nouv. série, No. 74 (July-August, 1957), pp. 32-48.

21. Lucien Goldmann, *The Hidden God,* transl. by Philip Thody (New York, 1964), p. 7.

22. Lucien Goldmann, *Pour une sociologie du roman* (Paris, 1964), p. 219.

23. Claude Lévi-Strauss, *Anthropologie structurale* (Paris, 1958), p. 306. For Taine, see p. 36 above.

24. Wellek, p. 57.

25. Serge Doubrovsky, *Pourquoi la nouvelle critique: Critique et objectivité* (Paris, 1966), pp. 181-82.

Selected Bibliography

PRIMARY SOURCES

On the publication history of Taine's works and the circumstances surrounding their writing the best, and most convenient source, is S. J. Kahn, pp. 247-61. For a list of Taine's articles, a number of which were not published in his three volumes of collected *Essais*, see A. Laborde-Milaà, *Hippolyte Taine: Essai d'une biographie intellectuelle* (Paris: Perrin, 1909), pp. 216-17 and 219-23. Listed below are Taine's major works only. Dates following the title are those of the first French edition. Dates and editions in parentheses indicate the edition used in this study. Unless otherwise stated, the publisher is Hachette, Paris.

1. *Essai sur les fables de La Fontaine*. Paris: Joubert, 1853.
    a. *La Fontaine et ses fables*. 1861 (17th ed.; 1905).
2. *Voyage aux Eaux des Pyrénées*. 1855.
    a. *Voyage aux Pyrénées*. 3d ed.; 1860.
3. *Essai sur Tite-Live*. 1856 (7th ed.; 1904).
4. *Les Philosophes français du XIXᵉ siècle*. 1857.
    a. *Les Philosophes classiques du XIXᵉ siècle*. 3d ed.; 1868 (9th ed., 1905).
5. *Essais de critique et d'histoire*. 1858 (12th ed.; 1904).
6. *Histoire de la littérature anglaise*. 3 vols. 1863.
    a. Vol. IV. 1864.
    b. 3d ed.; 5 vols. 1873.
    c. 8th (definitive) ed.; 5 vols. 1892 (13th ed.; 1911).
7. *Philosophie de l'art*. 1865.
8. *Nouveaux essais de critique et d'histoire*. 1865 (12th ed.; 1905).
9. *Voyage en Italie*. 1866.
10. *Philosophie de l'art en Italie*. 1866.
11. *Notes sur Paris, vie et opinions de M. Frédéric-Thomas Graindorge*, docteur en philosophie de l'Université de Iena, principal associé commanditaire de la maison Graindorge and Co (Huiles et porc salé,

à Cincinnati, Etats-Unis d'Amérique). Recueillies et publiées par H. Taine, son exécuteur testamentaire. 1867.

12. *De l'Idéal dans l'art.* 1867.
13. *Philosophie de l'art dans les Pays-Bas.* 1868.
14. *Philosophie de l'art en Grèce.* 1869.
15. *De l'Intelligence.* 1870 (32d ed.; 1948).
16. *Notes sur l'Angleterre.* 1871.
17. *Du Suffrage universel et de la manière de voter.* 1871.
18. *Les Origines de la France contemporaine.* 1875-1893 (36th ed.; 1947).

    a. *L'Ancien Régime.* 1875.
    b. *La Révolution.* Vol. I: *L'Anarchie.* 1878. Vol. II: *La Conquête jacobine.* 1881. Vol. III: *Le Gouvernement révolutionnaire.* 1884.
    c. *Le Régime moderne.* Vol. I: 1891. Vol. II: 1894.

19. *Derniers essais de critique et d'histoire.* 1894 (1st ed.; 1894).
20. *Carnets de voyage: Notes sur la province (1863-1865).* 1896.
21. *H. Taine, sa vie et sa correspondance.* 4 vols. 1902-1907 (4th ed.; 1914).
22. *Etienne Mayran.* 1910.

English Translations

Numbers correspond to the listing above. Unless otherwise indicated, the publisher is New York: Holt.

2. *A Tour through the Pyrenees* (transl. by J. S. Fiske). 1876.
6. *History of English Literature* (transl. by H. Van Laun). 2 vols. 1872.
7. *Lectures on Art* (transl. by J. Durand). 2 vols. 1896. Contains 7, 10, 12, 13, and 14.
8. Only one essay translated. *Balzac: A Critical Study* (transl. by Lorenzo O'Rourke). New York: Funk and Wagnalls. 1906.
9. *Italy* (transl. by J. Durand).
    a. I: *Rome and Naples.* 1870.
    b. II: *Florence and Venice.* 1871.
11. *Notes on Paris* (transl. by J. A. Stevens). 1879.
15. *On Intelligence* (transl. by T. D. Haye). 2 vols. 1889.
16. *Notes on England* (transl. by W. F. Rae). 1885.
    a. (transl. by E. Hyams). Fairlawn, N. J.: Essential Books. 1958.
18. *The Origins of Contemporary France* (transl. by J. Durand).
    a. *The Ancient Regime.* 1885 (London: Low, Marston, Searle and Kivington. 1881).

b. *The French Revolution.* Vol. I: 1897. Vol. II: 1892. Vol. III: 1885.

c. *The Modern Regime.* 2 vols. 1890-1894.

20. *Journeys Through France, Being Impressions of the Provinces* (anonymous transl.). 1897.

21. *Life and Letters* of H. Taine. 3 vols. 1902-1908.

a. Vols. I and II: (transl. by Mrs. R. L. Devonshire).

b. Vol. III: (abridged and transl. by E. Sparvel-Bayly).

SECONDARY SOURCES

The literature about Taine is so extensive that it is impossible to do it justice in the confines of this study. The bibliography below indicates where the material can be found, in chronological order.

THIEME, HUGO P. "The Development of Taine Criticism since 1893," *Modern Language Notes,* XVII (1902), 71-82, 140-53.

————. *Bibliographie de la littérature française de 1800 à 1930.* Paris: Droz, 1933, II, 835-45.

SMITH, H. "The Taine Centennial: Comment and Bibliography," *Modern Language Notes,* XLIV (1929), 437-45.

DREHER, S. and M. ROLLI, *Bibliographie de la littérature française de 1930 à 1939.* Lille: Giard; Geneva: Droz, 1948, p. 396.

DREVET, MARGUERITE L. *Bibliographie de la littérature française de 1940 à 1949.* Geneva: Droz; Lille: Giard, 1954, p. 585.

Books and Articles

Included are only those works that are either standard references or that offer a particularly helpful and interesting view on Taine. Much of the excluded material is in the notes.

AULARD, A. *Taine historien de la Révolution française.* Paris: Colin, 1907. Attacks Taine's study of the French Revolution by accusing him of prejudice and of improper documentation.

BARZELOTTI, GIACOMO. *La Philosophie de Taine* (transl. from the Italian by A. Dietrich). Paris: Alcan, 1900. A book full of solid information based on a careful study of Taine's philosophy; however, the author is a Kantian and at times judges Taine on that basis.

BOURGET, PAUL. *Essais de psychologie contemporaine.* Paris: Lemerre, 1885, pp. 175-220. A close associate of Taine who sees in him primarily the philosopher.

BOUTMY, EMILE. *Taine, Scherer, Laboulaye.* Paris: Colin, 1901, pp. 1-49. A good friend of Taine's who sees in his work a conservative and Classical profession of faith.

BRUNETIERE, FERDINAND. *L'Evolution des genres dans l'histoire de la littérature*. Paris: Hachette, 1898, I, pp. 245-78. Generally respectfully critical of Taine but praises his idea of moment.

CHEVRILLON, ANDRE. *Taine: Formation de sa pensée*. Paris: Plon, 1932. A key book on Taine by his nephew who was his direct intellectual heir.

──────. *Portrait de Taine—Souvenirs*. Paris: Fayard, 1958. Valuable information on Taine's verbal explanations of his ideas revealed by his nephew.

CRESSON, ANDRE. *Hippolyte Taine: Sa Vie, son oeuvre*. Paris: Presses Universitaires, 1951. Information on Taine brought up-to-date. Excellent section on *On Intelligence*.

DUTOIT, EUGENE. *Die Theorie des Milieu*. Bern: Sturzenegger, 1898. Dissertation on development of milieu theory from Aristotle to Taine, showing Taine's contribution but criticizing him for not realizing mutual influence of milieu and man.

EUSTIS, ALVIN A. *Hippolyte Taine and the Classical Genius*. Berkeley and Los Angeles: University of California Press, 1951. A firstrate monograph on this important part of Taine's work, distinguished by good judgment and a maximum of information in a minimum of space. Good bibliography.

GIBAUDAN, RENE. *Les Idées sociales de Taine*. Paris: Argo, 1928. Good study on Taine's philosophical and sociological views, method, and influence.

GIRAUD, VICTOR. *Essai sur Taine: Son Oeuvre et son influence*. Paris: Hachette, 1901. Pioneer work on Taine. Excellent information, but author is obviously ill at ease in dealing with Taine's religious and deterministic views and tries to softpedal them.

──────. *Hippolyte Taine: Etudes et documents*. Paris: Vrin, 1928. Stresses Taine's Romanticism. Contains unpublished letters and selections from articles not contained in the various *Essays*.

KAHN, SHOLOM J. *Science and Aesthetic Judgment: A Study in Taine's Critical Method*. London: Routledge and Kegan Paul, 1953. A "must" for philosophical and methodological information but not always easy reading.

LABORDE-MILAA, A. *H. Taine: Essai d'une biographie intellectuelle*. Paris: Perrin, 1909. Explains the underlying purpose of Taine's work (as opposed to titles of his books). Good section on master faculty. Appendix contains list of all articles by Taine.

LACOMBE, PAUL. *La Psychologie des individus et des sociétés chez Taine historien des littératures*. Paris: Alcan, 1906. Critical and effective examination of Taine's *History of English Literature*.

Denies that Taine demonstrated persistence of English racial traits.

——. *Taine historien et sociologue.* Paris: Girard et Brière, 1909. Denies Taine's charge that the French Revolution was based on an abstract view of man and criticizes his solutions, but defends him against the label of reactionary by concluding Taine was a liberal.

LEROY, MAXIME. *Taine.* Paris: Rieder, 1933. Good study of family life, friends of Taine and of the intellectual atmosphere of the period.

MARGERIE, AMEDEE DE. *H. Taine.* Paris: Poussielgue, 1894. Good analysis of Taine's style and of his study of La Fontaine.

MONOD, GABRIEL. *Les Maîtres de l'histoire: Renan, Taine, Michelet.* Paris: Calmann-Lévy, 1894, pp. 50-173. Demonstrates phases and unity of Taine's thought. Contains accurate information about his life.

MORAWSKI, STEFAN. "The Problem of Value and Criteria in Taine's Aesthetics," *Journal of Aesthetics and Art Criticism,* XXI (1963), 407-21. A thorough study of Taine's *Ideal in Art,* exposing clearly the basic views and inconsistencies in Taine's criteria.

NEVE, PAUL. *La Philosophie de Taine: Essai critique.* Paris: Lecoffre; Brussels: Dewit, 1908. Traces influence of Spinoza in Taine's work; good analysis of *On Intelligence.*

PETROVICH, O. *H. Taine historien littéraire du XVIIe siècle.* Paris: Bonvalot-Jouve, 1907. Sorbonne dissertation criticizing Taine for imposing too much uniformity on the Classical century. Less thorough than Eustis.

RICE, WINTHROP H. "The Meaning of Taine's *Moment,*" *Romanic Review,* XXX (1939), 273-79. Finds Taine's "moment" almost useless, since it is made up of the effects of race and milieu.

ROE, F. C. *Taine et l'Angleterre.* Paris: Champion, 1923. Information on Taine's trips to England. Criticizes his method in *History of English Literature* as an attempt to prove preconceived ideas of English character and accuses him of not distinguishing between English and Scottish writers.

ROSCA, D. D. *L'Influence de Hegel sur Taine théoricien de la connaissance et de l'art.* Paris: J. Gamber, 1928. Shows influence of Hegel on Taine and in which respects the two differed. Recommended for philosophical background reading on Taine.

SAINT-RENE TAILLANDIER, G. *Auprès de M. Taine.* Paris: Hachette, 1928. Taine's nephew by marriage describes his discussions with his uncle.

SCHAEPDRYVER, K. DE. *Hippolyte Taine: Essai sur l'unité de sa pensée.* Paris: Droz, 1938. Defends thesis that Taine's ideas were the same before 1870 as after, i.e., that the War of 1870 and the Commune did not cause a sudden change in his views.

WELLEK, RENE. *A History of Modern Criticism, 1750-1950.* New Haven and London: Yale University Press, 1965, IV, 27-57. Appeared previously in *Criticism,* I (1959), 1-18, 123-38. A masterful analysis of Taine's criticism, especially strong on *History of English Literature* and on the way Taine dealt with style.

WHITE, JOHN S. "Taine on Race and Genius," *Social Research* X (February, 1943), 76-99. Sees in Taine the condemnation of the civilized man of the seventeenth, eighteenth, and nineteenth centuries, and shows the development of this trend from Lessing and Herder to Taine.

WIARDA, R. *Taine et la Hollande.* Paris: Droz, 1938. Valuable information on Taine's relationship with Camille Selden, on critical opponents of Taine, and on his treatment of Dutch art.

WOLFENSTEIN, MARTHA. "The Background of Taine's Philosophy of Art," *Journal of the History of Ideas,* V (1944), 332-58. Attacks and shows inconsistencies in Taine's historical relativism. Links his attitude to the dilemma of being unable to free himself from the laws of bourgeois society while recognizing its decline.

ZEITLER, JULIUS. *Die Kunstphilosophie von Hippolyte Adolphe Taine.* Leipzig, Seemann, 1901. Accuses Taine of using works of art not for their intrinsic value but as historical documents.

Index

Note: Italics are used to indicate chief entries.

About, Edmond, 18, 154
Abstraction, 25, 31, 34, 42, 108, 132-33, 145, 156, 173
Acton, John Emerich Edward Dalberg-, 141
Adler, Alfred, 44
Aeschylus, 119
Age, 35, 36, 40, 74, 96, 150; spirit of the, 28-29, 40, 53, 56, 66, 75, 80, 98, 103, 122, 126, 127, 136, 143, 150; *see also* French Seventeenth Century
America, *see* United States of America
Amiel, H. F., 25
Analogy, 35
Analysis, *32-33,* 52, 55, 86
Ancien Régime, 23, 124, 125, 126, 128, 133, 135, 136, 137, 139, 167
Anselm, Saint, 67
Anthropology, 148
Aquinas, Saint Thomas, 67
Architecture, 100, 101, 102, 165
Aristotle, 29, 42, 120, 157
Art, 17, 25, 29, 39, 50, 54, 96, 97, 122, 143, 144; and health, 118; and morality, 116-18, 120; and nature, 119; and religion, 115; and society, 101, 144; as historical document, 174; conditions for great, 103-4, 106, 112; in Greece, 106, 107-9. 112, 118; in Italy, 105-7, 112, 115, 119, 144; in the Netherlands, 106, 109-11; *see also* Taine, *Lectures on Art;* individual arts
Artist, 26, 35, 37, 38, 71, 75, 104; and society, 51, 98, 104; great, 112, 116
Astronomy, 40, 43
Augier, Emile, 146
Augustine, Saint, 67
Aulard, A., 140

Bacon, Sir Francis, 160
Baldensperger, Ferdinand, 147-48
Balzac, Honoré de, 26, 55, *57-60,* 62, 63, 87, 98, 116, 117, 119, 120, 121, 144, 146, 148, 150, 159, 160, 161; and Taine, 57; master faculty, 58; mysticism, 59-60; society in, 59; style, 59
Barrès, Maurice, 145, 155
Barthes, Roland, 148
Baudelaire, Charles, 147, 168

Beaumarchais, Pierre Augustin Caron, 114

Beethoven, Ludwig van, 113

Bergson, Henri, and Taine, 147

Bernard, Claude, 16, 34

Berthelot, Marcelin, 16. 23, 155

Biran, Maine de; *see* Maine de Biran

Blanc, Louis, 167

Body, and soul, 116; athletic, 108, 116; human, 104, 110, 119; nude, 108, 118

Boileau-Despréaux, Nicolas, 36, 65, 69, 78

Bonald, Louis de, 163

Bossuet, Jacques Bénigne, 31, 36, 67, 119, 155

Botany, 40, 127

Bourdaloue, Louis, 67

Bourget, Paul, 23, 145, 146, 155

Brandès, Georges, 27

Bronowski, J., 148

Browning, Elizabeth Barrett, 163

Browning, Robert, 163

Brunetière, Ferdinand, 17, 145, 147 167

Buchez, Philippe, 124

Buddhism, 83

Buffon, Georges Louis Leclerc de, 127

Bunyan, John, 86

Burckhardt, Jakob, 97, 154

Butler, Samuel, 114

Byron, George Gordon, 26, 86, *93-94*, 98. 117, 119, 144; and Goethe, 93

Calderón de la Barca, Pedro, 114

Calvin, John, and Calvinists, 38; style, 161

Camus, Albert, 98-99

Caracci Brothers, 119

Carlyle, Thomas, 88, 89, 94, 124, 144

Carrier, Jean-Baptiste, 130, 134

Catholicism and Catholic, 24, 139

Cause, 28, *32,* 34, 35, 36, 37, 39, 41, 42, 53, 54, 56, 57, 64, 66, 85, 116, 122, 123, 125, 141, 150; and effect, 32, 51, 52, 135, 151; dominant, 43; first, 42; race as, 81; *see also* Force and Forces, generative

Cavendish, Henry, 127

Cazamian, Louis, 145

Cellini, Benvenuto, 106

Champmeslé (la), Marie Desmares, 70

Character, basic, of race, 75; beneficence in, 112, 113, *116-18*, 120, 135, 144, 146; importance of, 112, *113-15*, 116, 118; subordination of, 35; universality of, 113

Charles V, 86

Chemistry, 40, 43, 127

Chevrillon, André, 43, 84, 153

Christianity, 24, 83

Church, *see* Catholicism and Catholic

Cicero, Marcus Tullius, 56, 116

Cimabue, Giovanni, 115

Civilization, 150; Italian, 83

Classic and Classical, 76. 89, 92, 93, 99, 123, 126, 127, 129, 132, 133, 145, 146, 162; method, 67; *see also* French Classical Theater, French Seventeenth Century

Clement of Alexandria, 132

Climate, 61, 81, 82, 83, 107, 115; intellectual and moral, 85, 100, 101-2, 106, 125, 141

Colbert, Jean-Baptiste, 36

Commodus, 116
Commune Uprising, 22, 124, 174
Comte, Auguste, 17, 30
Condillac, Etienne Bonnot, abbé
de, 33, 158
Conditions, 34, 77-78, 123, 149;
for great art, 103-4, 106, 112
Convergence, of effects, 118-120
Corneille, Pierre, 22, 58, 63, 65,
69, 72, 78, 84, 117; his
psychology, 68
Corneille, Thomas, 65
Courbet, Gustave, 146
Cousin, Victor, 17, 20, *30-31*;
style, 31
Crayer, Gaspard de, 118
Criticism and Critics, 143, 148;
and the novel, 53; Bergsonian,
148; literary, 20, 52, 98;
"new," 148; *see also* Taine, as
art critic; Taine, as literary
critic
Cromwell, Oliver, 118
Cuvier, Georges, 35, 57

Dadaism, 147
Dante Alighieri, 102, 113, 114,
119
Danton, Georges Jacques, *130-
31, 132*
Darwin, Charles, 16, 35
Daudet, Alphonse, 146
Decadence, 101, 119, 123
Deduction, 32, 41, 44, 65, 77,
159; *see also* Induction
Delacroix, Ferdinand Victor
Eugène, 119
Delille, Jacques, 65
De Mabuse, Jan, 105
Dependencies, 34, 108, 149
Descartes, René, 29, 78, 98;
criticized, 67, 69, 156, 161;

his psychology, 68
Determinism, 35, 36, 59, 73, 112,
136, 172; and morality, 38,
121
De Vos, Martin, 105, 120
De Witt, Jakob, 105
Dialectics, 103
Dickens, Charles, 87, *94-95*;
master faculty, 94
Diderot, Denis, master faculty, 64
Diocletian, 116
Don Quixote, 114, 115, 116, 117
Doubrovsky, Serge, 150
Dreyfus Affair, 24
Droz, François-Xavier-Joseph,
167
Dryden, John, 84, 119
Dumas the Elder, Alexandre,
69, 114
Dumas the Younger, Alexandre,
146
Duns Scotus, John, 31
Du Parc, Marquise Thérèse de
Gorla, 70
Durability, as criterion in art,
112-13
Dürer, Albrecht, 113, 117

Eclecticism, 17, 30, 32; *see also*
Philosophers, eclectic
Ecole des Beaux-Arts, 20, 44, 164
Ecole Normale, 17, 18, 29, 44
Education, 24, 25, 31, 53, 114,
133
Eggleston, Edward, 145
Ego, 30, 46, 151
Eliot, George, 163
Emotions, *see* Passion
England and English, 22, 25, 42,
82, 87, 115, 138-39; morality,
95-96; national character, 40,
80, 93, 95, 97, 100, 173;

philosophy and philosophers, 67, 95; Restoration, 87, 92, 105, 161, 164; Renaissance, 104, 108; painters, 114; religion, 95; wit, 91
Epoch, *see* Age
Esthetics, 39, 87, 99, 143, 144
Euripides, 119
Experience, 127, 156
Experiment, 16, 156
Expressionism, 147

Facts, 16, 42, 127
Faculty and Faculties, dominant; *see* Master Faculty
Faguet, Emile, 55, 150
Faure, Elie, 145
Fénelon, François de Salignac de la Mothe-, 67
Fielding, Henry, 86, 89, 116
Flanders and Flemish, art, 106, 109-11; painting, 105, 109-10, 119, 145; Renaissance, 104
Flaubert, Gustave, 21, 116, 143, 146; on hallucination, 158; style, 162
Floris, Franz, 105, 120
Force and Forces, 36; generative, 86
Formula and Formulas, 26, 39, 43, 56, 57, 64, 98, 99, 120, 131, 148; Taine's, 35, 102, 157, 160
Fornarina, la (model of Raphael), 97
Fra Angelico (Giovanni da Fiesole), 117, 119
Fra Bartolommeo, 118
France, Anatole, 17, 146
France and French, 40, 74, 75, 78, 82, 87, 115, 124, 147; clergy, 125, 136; commoners, 126; history, 122-42; national character, 78, 123; nobles, 125, 126, 128, 136, 138, 139; painting, 107; peasants, 125; philosophers, 78; tragedies, 117; wit, 91; workers, 125; *see also* French Classical Theater, French Revolution, French Seventeenth Century, Gallic Spirit and Tradition, Paris, and *passim*
Franco-Prussian War, 21, 174
Freedom, 31, 35, 36
French Academy, 20, 22, 56, 147
French Classical Theater, 68-69
French Revolution, 23, 26, 49, 65, 78, 98, 124, 125, *128-39*, 140-42, 144, 148, 151, 171, 173; atrocities, 134; causes, 66, 125; criticism of, 132-35; master passion, 128; *see also* individual revolutionaries
French Seventeenth Century, 26, 41, 49, 56, 61, 63, *65-68*, 84, 90, 105, 114, 144, 151, 173; authors, 77, 79, 161; conditions of, 77-78; master faculty, 69, 72, 79; spirit, 66, 67, 69, 75, 78, 136; Taine's dislike of, 28; theater, 68-69, 161
Fréron, Louis-Marie Stanislas, 130, 134
Freud, Sigmund, and Freudians, 28, 44, 145, 159; and Taine compared, 46

Gallic Spirit and Tradition, 74-75, 131, 162
Gautier, Théophile, 21, 165
Genetics, 148
Genius, 140; Taine on, 85-86, 161

Geoffroy Saint-Hilaire, Etienne, 57

Geoffroy Saint-Hilaire, Isidore, 20

Geology, 36

Geometry, 36

Germany and Germans, 4, 82, 107, 147, 163; national character, 93; painting, 35, 107; philosophers, 67; *see also* Race, Germanic

Gifford, John, 141

Giotto di Bondone, 102, 119

Giraud, Victor, 160

Gödel, Kurt, 148, 168

Goethe, Johann Wolfgang von, 26, 114, 118; and Byron, 93

Goldmann, Lucien, 149

Goncourt Brothers, 21, 153

Goya Lucientes, Francisco de, 165

Greece and Greek, 22, 83, 87, 151; tragedies, 117; *see also* Art, in Greece; Sculpture, Greek

Guérard, Sr., Albert L., 145

Guido, Reni, 119

Guizot, François, 159

Guizot, Guillaume, 62

Hachette (publisher), 19

Hallucination, 47, 90, 91; Flaubert on, 158

Havet, Ernest, 36

Health, 48; and art, 118

Hegel, G. F. W., 17, 19, 20, 29, 31, 41, 42, 103, 151, 157, 173

Heine, Heinrich, 26, 27

Hennequin, Emile, 164

Herder, Johann Gottfried, 174

Hérédia, José-Maria de, 23, 155

Heredity, 73, 81, 98

Hicks, Granville, 145

History and Historians, 25, 29, 36, 40, 43, 50, 53, 57, 67, 86, 94, 96, 144, 145; and literature, 84; French, 122-42; of a people, 39; *see also* Taine, as historian

Hobbes, Thomas, 49, 139

Hogarth, William, 114

Holland and Dutch, 105; art, 106, 109-11; painting, 105, 110-11, 145

Hollard, H. (pastor), 24

Homer, 115, 118

Honnête homme, 66, 126

Horace, 61

Howells, William Dean, 145

Hugo, Victor, 69, 72, 114, 117, 154

Huizinga, Johan, 96

Hulst, Monsignor d', 24

Humanities, *see* Science and Sciences, human

Hume, David, 158

Hypothesis, 34

Idea and Ideas, 112, 157; and images, 107

Ideal Man, 39, 56, 66, 80, 96, 97, 98, 100, 102, 103, 126, 165; Taine's, 22

Ideologists, 25

Images, 55; and ideas, 107; and sensations, 107; spontaneous, 104

Imitation of Christ, 115

Induction, 40, 42, 64; inductive-deductive method, 40, 64; *see also* Deduction

Intelligence, and imagination, 52; Taine's definition of, 44

Intuition, 25, 147

Italy and Italian, 95, 97, 104, 115, 165; *see also* Art, in Italy; Painting and Painters, Italian; Renaissance, Italian

Jacobins, 125, *128-32*, 134, 140
Jacquinet, Paul, 18-19
Jansenism and Jansenists, 67, 69
Johnson, Samuel, 92-93
Jonson, Ben, 92
Jordaens, Jacob, 118
Jouffroy, Théodore, 30, 31
Joyce, James, 77
Jung, Carl Gustav, 44
Jusserand, J. J. 145

Kant, Immanuel, and Kantians, 19, 41, 44, 47, 51, 171; criticized, 158
Knowledge, Taine's theory of, 44ff.

La Bruyère, Jean, 65, 67, 69, 161
Lacombe, Paul, 140
La Fayette, Mme. de, 65, 69, *70-71;* style, 70-71
La Fontaine, Jean de, 69, 70, 119, 162; as ideal poet, 76; as representative artist, 74-75; style, 77, 161
Lamarck, Chevalier Jean Baptiste Pierre Antoine de Monet de, 127
Lamartine, Alphonse de, 167
La Mettrie, Julien de, 34
Lanson, Gustave, 147
Lapp. John C., 146
La Rochefoucauld, François de, 65, 69
La Rochefoucauld-Liancourt, Francois de, 137
Latin, 75, 82, 162, 163; *see also* Race, Latin

Lavisse, Ernest, 23, 155
Lavoisier, Antoine-Laurent, 127
Law and Laws, 34, 35, 36, 37, 54, 63, 86, 122, 123, 144, 150; first, 42, 43
Leibnitz, Gottfried Wilhelm von, 31, 38, 41, 44-45
Lemaître, Jules, 55, 150
Lesage, Alain-René, 114
Lessing, Gotthold Ephraim, 109, 165, 174
Lesueur, Eustache, 119
Linguistics, 148
Linnaeus, Carolus, 127
Literature, 17, 25, 29, 50, 53, 54, 113, 122, 143, 144, 145; and history, 84; and painting, 107; and philosophy, 96; and society, 99, 145; as document, 51, 54, 85, 143; comparative, 86-87; world, 150
Livy, Titus, 55, *56-57*, 155; master faculty, 41, 56
Locke, John, 44
Lombard, Lambert, 105
Lope de Vega Carpio, 114
Louis XIV, 23, 40, 65, 75, 78, 84, 87, 105, 126, 139; age of, 36, 75
Louis XVI, 118, 137
Louis-Bonaparte, *see* Napoleon III
Louis-Napoleon, *see* Napoleon III
Loyola, Saint Ignatius of, 97
Luther, Martin, 97
Lyly, John, 114

Macaulay, Thomas, 88, 93, 144, 163
Madness, 47, 48, 68, 73, 90, 91

Maine de Biran, Marie-François-Pierre, *30-31*

Maintenon, Marquise de, 70

Malebranche, Nicolas de, 36

Malherbe, François de, 65

Mallet du Pan, Jacques, 141

Malouet, Pierre-Victor, 141

Man, 39, 127; Classical conception of, 126, 132; Rousseau's conception of, 127; Taine's conception of, 34, 44, 48, 49, 89, 91

Manicheans, 60

Marat, Jean-Paul, *130*, 132

Marcus Aurelius, 26

Marx, Karl, and Marxist Critics, 145, 148, 149

Masaccio, Tommaso Guidi, 115

Master Faculty, 29, 36, 38, 40, 51, 54, 77, 80, 85, 98, 100, 112, 130, 148, 150, 160; defined, 56-57; evaluated, 63-65; of an age, 56; Taine's concept of, 35; *see also* French Revolution, French Seventeenth Century, individual authors

Mathematics, 29, 43, 165

Mathilde Bonaparte, Princess, 21, 23, 140

Maupassant, Guy de, 146

Mauron, Charles, 148, 162

Maurras, Charles, 24

Maximilian, 86

Measurement, 16, 36, 46, 50, 84; instruments of, 33, 43, 44, 120

Mechanics and Mechanical, 43, 46, 84, 126

Memling, Hans, 117

Metaphysics, 18, 33, 67, 78, 83, 93, 107; Taine's 41-43

Method, 18, *30-31*, 32, 34, 37, 40, 52, 53, 127, 144; Descartes',

29; Taine's, *34-41*, 44, 51, 65, 79, 90, 98, 99, 100, 123, 135, 141, 143, 144, 147, 150, 156, 161, 165, 172; *see also* Scientific Method

Metzu, Gabriel, 105

Michelangelo Buonarroti, 97, 101, 113, 118, 119, 151

Michelet, Jules, 86, 89, 141-42, 163, 167; master faculty, 64

Middle Ages, 96, 99, 113, 114

Mignet, François-Auguste-Marie, 167

Milieu, 61, 81, *82-83*, 94, 95, 98, 106, 123, 148, 172

Mill, John Stuart, 29, 40, 42, 94, 156, 158

Milton, John, 144

Mirabeau, Comte Honoré Gabriel Victor Riqueti de, 118, 139, 141

Molière, J.-B. P., 65, 69, 70, 75, 87, 116, 162

Moment, *83-84*, 123, 163, 173

Monnier, Henri, 116, 146

Montaigne, Michel de, 159, 160; style, 161

Montesquieu, Baron Charles de, 159, 163

Montfleury, Zacharie Jacob, 73

Moral and Morality, 36, 59, 66, 74, 96, 118, 135, 146, 166; and art, 116-18, 120; and determinism, 38, 121; and science, 31; English, 95-96

Mormons, 61

Morris, Governor, 141

Mozart, Wolfgang Amadeus, 113

Mulready, William, 114

Murillo, Bartolomé Esteban, 165

Music, 100, 101, 102, 165

Musset, Alfred de, 26, 87

Napoleon Bonaparte, 23, 60, 128, 135, *139-40,* 154; master faculty, 140

Napoleon III, 19

Nation and National, art, 105; basic traits, 114; English, 113, 122; French, 113, 122

Naturalism and Naturalists, 58, 112; French, 48, 59, 146, 150, 160

Nature, 39, 42, 47, 94, 101; and art, 119

Netherlands, *see* Holland and Dutch, Flanders and Flemish

New Régime, 125

Newton, Sir Isaac, 78, 127

Nicole, Pierre, 67

Niebelungenlied, 118

Nietzsche, Friedrich, 154

Novel and Novelists, 38; and criticism, 53

Observation, 127; instruments of, 98, 150

Oratory and Oratorical, 25, 26, 31, 67, 78, 84, 87, 126, 147

Orvieto, Pietro d', 104

Otway, Thomas, 92, 119

Owen, Richard, 35

Painting and Painters, 37, 100, 101, 113, 115, 118, 119; Dutch, 105, 110-11, 145; English, 114; Flemish, 105, 109-10, 119, 145; French, 107; German, 35, 107; Italian, 105, 106-7, 117, 120; Spanish, 115, 165

Pantheism, 18, 31, 43; Spinoza's, 41; Taine's, 42

Paris and Parisians, 19, 23, 58, 131, 160

Paris, Gaston, 23, 155

Parrington, Vernon L., 145

Pascal, Blaise, 69; as artist, 75; style, 161

Passion, 45, 62, 67, 70, 71, 72, 73, 77, 104, 109, 114, 117, 119; abstract, 77; violent, 59, 69, 70, 74, 78, 145

Perception, 30, 108, 151; Taine's theory of, *44-47*

Philosophers, eclectic, 26, 30-31; English, 67; French, 78; German, 67

Philosophy, 25, 39, 68, 88, 126, 127, 144, 145; and literature, 96; Taine's, *28-34,* 41-44, 147; *see also* Metaphysics

Physics, 40, 43, 46

Physiology, 36, 40, 45, 46, 50, 127, 148

Plato, 115

Plumptree, Anne, 141

Poetry and Poets, 37, 38, 68, 69, 71, 75, 100; lyrical, 77; Taine's definition of, 76

Politics, 67, 138; Taine's views on, 22, 24, 25, 27, 49, 61, 138

Pollaiolo, Antonio del, 117

Pope, Alexander, 160

Positivism, 17, 30, 32

Poussin, Nicolas, 119

Prévost d'Exiles, abbé, 114

Prévost-Paradol, Lucien A., 18, 19, 24, 154

Priestley, Joseph, 127

Protestantism and Protestants, 22, 24, 88, 96

Prud'hon, Pierre, 119

Psychiatry, 148

Psychology, 25, 28, 29, 31, 43, 67, 122, 125, 128, 143, 144, 145, 148; and literary criticism, 53; Taine's, *44-50;* Taine's

projected dissertation on, 19, 20
Pulci, Luigi, 97
Puritans, 38, 82, 96, 124

Quietism, 67

Rabelais, François, 75, 130
Race, 35, 36, 53, 73, 74, 75, *80-82*, 96, 98, 106, 107, 108, 115, 123, 143, 148, 150; Aryan, 81, 82, 113; as cause, 82; Germanic, 82, 83, *87-88*, 105, 145; Latin, 83, *87*, 88, 145; Semitic, 82, 113
Race-Milieu-Moment, 37, 40, 56, 65, *84-85*, 97, 98, 100, 112, 123, 132, 144, 145, 150
Racine, Jean, 22, 26, 65, *69-74*, 76, 78, 87, 114, 119, 126, 136, 141, 161, 162, 164; and Shakespeare, 61, 90; as national poet, 74; as representative artist, 75; characters, 72-73; contradictions in Taine's judgment of, 71; lack of passion, 69-70; life, 69, 162; love in, 72; master faculty, 64, 72; psychology, 68
Raphael (Sanzio), 97, 113, 118, 119
Reason, 18, 31, 49, 66, 68, 127, 136
Reigning Model, *see* Ideal Man
Religion, 25, 39, 54, 66, 107, 139; French Classical, 67; in art, 115; Taine's, 18, *24*, 139, 172
Rembrandt van Rijn, 105, *110-11*, 113, 117, 119, 151, 165
Renaissance, 82, 92, 97, 99, 102, 113, 115, 116, 117; English, 104, 108; Flemish, 104; Italian,

26, 61, 87, 103, 106, 107, 108, 115, 118, 135, 151
Renan, Ernest, 16, 23, 24, 145, 159
Renaud de Montauban, 119
Representative, art and artists, 35, 74-75, 98
Revel, Jean-François, 100
Revolution, French; *see* French Revolution
Rhetoric and Rhetorical, 26
Richards, I. A., 145
Richardson, Samuel, 89, 117
Richelieu, Cardinal Armand-Jean du Plessis, 139
Robespierre, Maximilien François Marie Isidore de, 78, 130, *131,* 132, 136, 166
Robinson Crusoe, 114, 115
Romanticism and Romantic, 16, 17, 69, 70, 72, 78, 88, 90, 93, 94, 154; French, 26, 114; Taine's, 69, 94, 172
Rousseau, Jean-Jacques, 78, 123, 127, 131, 132, 139; and Taine, 133; master faculty, 64
Roux-Lavergne, Pierre Célestin, 124
Royer-Collard, Pierre-Paul, 31
Rubens, Peter Paul, 101, *109-10*, 113, 115, 118, 119, 120, 121, 145
Ruskin, John, 163
Ruysch, Rachel, 105

Sainte-Beuve, Charles-Augustin, 18, 21, 52, 53, 54, 67, 73, 86, 121, 143, 147, 150, 159, 164; method of, 52-53
Saint-Hilaire, Geoffroy, *see* Geoffroy Saint-Hilaire
Saint-Just, Louis Antoine Léon

de, 78, 130, *131-32*

Saint-Simon, Comte Claude Henri de Rouvroy de, 65; as artist, 75; as ideal author, 76; master faculty, 64; style, 77

Sallust, Gaius Sallustius Crispus, 56

Sand, George, 21, 87, 117; master faculty, 64

Sarcey, Francisque, 18, 154

Sartre, Jean-Paul, 159

Saxons, 92

Scales of Value, 100, *112-20*

Scheele, Karl Wilhelm, 127

Scherer, Edmond, 106

Schlegel, Friedrich, 160

Science and the Sciences, 16, 28, 29, 40, 42, 83, 127, 145, 146, 147, 148, 150; and morality, 31; human and moral, 34, 36, 37, 43, 44, 51, 53, 65, 144, 150; natural, 29, 35, 102; physical, 29, 34, 37, 43, 44, 51, 53, 84, 144, 150; social, 129; *see also* individual sciences

Scientific Method, 17, 25, 26, 43, 127, 143, 144

Scientism, 147

Scientists, natural, 25, 86, 124

Scott, Sir Walter, master faculty, 94

Scudéry, Madeleine de, 114

Sculpture, 100, 101, 113; Greek, 118, 120

Selden, Camille, 153, 166, 174

Sensations. 26. 46, 83; and images, 107; Taine's projected dissertation on, 44

Sévigné, Marquise de, 69

Shakespeare, William, 26, 49, 69, 74, 86, 88, *89-92,* 93, 97, 109, 110, 113, 115, 117, 119, 120,

121, 141, 144, 151; and Hamlet, 91-92, and Racine, 61, 90; master faculty, 89; view of man, 90

Signorelli, Luca, 117

Skepticism, 31, 43

Snow, C. P., 150

Socialism, 24, 140

Society, and art, 101, 144; and artist, 51, 98, 104; and literature, 99, 145; in Balzac, 59; Rousseau's theoretical, 133

Sociology, 145, 148

Song of Roland, 118, 119, 120

Sophocles, 69, 74, 119

Spain and Spanish. Golden Age, 114; painters, 115, 165; tragedies, 117

Spencer, Herbert, 158

Spinoza, Baruch, and Spinozism, 19, 20, 29, 38, 41, 42, 45, 61, 151, 156, 158, 173; pantheism, 41

Spirit of the Times, *see* Age, spirit of the

Spiritualism, *see* Eclecticism

Staël, Mme. Anne Louise Germaine de, 87, 163

Stahl, Georg Ernst, 127

State of Mind, *see* Climate, intellectual and moral

Stendhal, 19, 26, 41, 55, *60-63,* 75, 95, 98, 99, 102, 121, 141, 144, 146, 150, 151, 159, 163; and Taine, 61; characters, 62-63; master faculty, 62-63; style, 62

Stoics, 38

Strauss, Claude Lévi, 149-150

Structuralism, 149

Style, 38, 42, 99, 119, 145, 161; *see also* individual authors

Suckau, Edouard de, 18, 154
Surrealism, 147
Swedenborg, Emanuel, 60
Symbolism and Symbolists, 147
Synthesis, 31, 34
System and Systems, 18, 39, 148;
 philosophical, 107

Tacitus, Cornelius, 56
Taine, Hippolyte-Adolphe,
 achievements, 143-44, 150-151;
 and Balzac, 57; and Bergson,
 147; and French Naturalism,
 48, 58-59, 146, 150; and
 Rousseau, 133; and Stendhal,
 61; and Zola, 146-47; as art
 critic, 28, 44, *100-121*, 122,
 144; as historian, 28, 44, 78,
 122-42, 151; as literary critic,
 28, *51-78*, 122, 143-44, 151,
 174; as philosopher, *28-34*,
 41-44, 147, 151; as psychologist, 28, *44-50*, 77, 78, 151; as
 scientist, 81; as teacher, 19, 21;
 birth, 17; burial place, 24;
 character, 24-25; contradictions
 in, 17, 36, 65, 71, 75-76, 77,
 82, 102-3, 109, 174; country
 home, 23, 24; death, 15, 24;
 disciples, 24; elected to French
 Academy, 22; enters Ecole
 Normale, 18; fails *agrégation*
 examination, 19, 20, 30, 61;
 family, 16; friends, 23, 24;
 influence of, 24, *145-50;*
 influence on, 29, 173; last will,
 15; life, 17-24; marriage, 21,
 166; master faculty, 16, mind,
 25, 145; political beliefs, 22,
 24, 25, 27, 49, 61, 138; religious
 beliefs, 18, *24*, 139, 172;
 Romanticism, 69, 94, 172;

 style, 25, 54-55, 173, 174;
 tensions in, 55; titles of works,
 54-55; travels, 21, 154-55, 165,
 173; *see also* Man, Taine's
 conception of; Master Faculty,
 Method, and *passim*

WORKS DISCUSSED:

Ancien Régime, The, 23, 65, 125
Critical and Historical Essays, 93;
 Prefaces, 52, 55, 86, 144, 156
Etienne Mayran, 21, 61
History of English Literature, 20,
 25, 65, 75, 80, 82, *86-99*, 100,
 105, 120, 121, 141, 155, 172,
 174; criticized, 173; Introduc-
 tion, 40, 80-84, 85, 144;
 purpose, 55
Ideal in Art, The, *112-21*, 144,
 146, 173
La Fontaine, 65, 74, 144, 173;
 dissertation, 19, 44; purpose,
 55
Lectures on Art, *100-121*, 136,
 144; *see also* Art, in Greece;
 Art, in Italy; Art, in the
 Netherlands; *Ideal in Art, The*
Livy, Essay on, 20, 34-35, *56-57*,
 122; purpose, 55
*Nineteenth Century Classical
 Philosophers, The*, 20, *30-34*,
 44, 156
'Of Human Destiny,' 17
On Intelligence, 21, 28, 43, *44-48*,
 131, 156, 172, 173
*Origins of Contemporary France,
 The*, 22, 23, 40, *122-42; see
 also Ancien Régime;* French
 Revolution, New Régime;
 Taine, *Ancien Régime, The*
Philosophy of Art, The, 17; *see
 also* Taine, *Lectures on Art*

Travel Books, 19, 154; Italy, 106, 112

Taine, Jean-Baptiste-Antoine (Taine's father), 17

Taine, Mme. (Taine's wife), 21, 153

Taine, Marie-Virginie (Taine's mother), 17

Taine, Pierre (Taine's great-grandfather), 17

Taine, Sophie (Taine's sister), 17

Taine, Virginie (Taine's sister), 17

Tarski, Alfred, 148

Tennyson, Alfred, 87, 118

Terburg, Gerard, 105

Thackeray, William, 87

Thibaudet, Albert, 147

Thiers, Adolphe, 167

Titian, 113

Tocqueville, Alexis de, 125, 167

Toynbee, Arnold J., 125, 141

Tradition, 136

Turgenev, Ivan Sergevich, 21

United States of America. 25, 61, 139, 145

Unity, 35, 51, 57, 173; of composition, 35

Urfé, Honoré d', 114

Value. 100; *see also* Scales of Value

Van Buren, Martin, 61

Van Huysum, Jan, 105

Van Oost, Jacob, 119-20

Van Orley, Bernard, 105, 119-20

Van Ruysdael, Jacob. 119

Van Thulden, Theodor, 118

Velásquez. Diego Rodriguez de Silva, 165

Venius, Otto, 120

Verification, 34

Verlaine, Paul, 168

Verrocchio, Andrea, 117

Vinci, Leonardo da, 102, 113, 119

Viollet-le-Duc, Eugène-Emmanuel, 20

Vogüé, Eugène Melchior de, 23, 153, 155

Voiture, Vincent, 74

Voltaire (François-Marie Arouet), 30, 75, 78, 84, 91, 115, 119, 127; master faculty, 64

Warton, Tomas, 163

Weber, Jean-Paul, 148

Wellek, René, 150, 163

White, John S., 91

Wilkie, Sir David, 114

Will. 31, 45, 58, 68; Taine's theory on, 159

Winckelmann, Johann Joachim, 108, 109, 165

Wordsworth, William, master faculty, 94

Writer and Writers, 26, 35, 37, 38, 69; great, 85-86, 100

Wundt, Wilhelm, 21

Wycherley, William, 84, 92

Young, Arthur, 141

Zola, Emile, 59; and Taine, 146-47

Zoology, 40, 43, 127